I often get annoyed when people are cle[...]
with it. Probably because I'm maturing. [...]
more than clever. It's helpful. It's deep. It's practical. It has perspective. Aaron
Sharp has given us the whole preggie/parent package, great for anyone in the
thick of it as well as those of us who love a host of chucklesome reminders.

Rhonda Rhea
award-winning humor columnist, TV personality, and author of
Fix Her Upper, Messy to Meaningful, Unruffled,
and *Off-Script & Over-Caffeinated*

If you're a new dad or about to be one—or you know someone who is—buy
this book. It's not only a fun and breezy read, it's chock-full of incredibly helpful information.

Drs. Les & Leslie Parrott
#1 *New York Times* bestselling authors of
Saving Your Marriage Before It Starts

New Dad Alert: Read this book the moment the pregnancy test comes back
positive. You will laugh, laugh, laugh. And (don't be alarmed) you will *learn* in
the process, becoming the husband and father your family needs.

Jay Payleitner
national speaker and bestselling author of
52 Things Kids Need from a Dad, 52 Ways to Connect as a Couple,
and *The Jesus Dare*

You Got This, Dad is a must-read for any wide-eyed man sailing into the
unchartered waters of a wife's pregnancy. My dear friend Aaron draws from
years of personal experience to deliver a practical, funny, honest, and encouraging portrayal of the crucial nine months leading to the birth of a couple's
baby. Aaron uses wit and humor to paint a realistic picture of what to expect in

this season of life. And in case you think it's just a man's opinion, his wonderful wife chimes in with hilarious footnotes throughout to add her viewpoint along the way. This engaging book is chock-full of helpful hints to help any man ease into this daunting assignment in life.

Afshin Ziafat
lead pastor, Providence Church, Frisco, TX

Thrilled, disoriented, terrified…those are just a few of the emotional states you'll pass through upon hearing you're going to be a father. Don't worry; Aaron Sharp is here to guide you. He's the big brother we all wish we had: honest, hilarious, and wise. His insider tips on fatherhood will make sure you're prepared (well, as much as you can be) when your little one arrives. This father of three highly recommends it!

Drew Dyck
author of *Your Future Self Will Thank You:*
Secrets to Self-Control from the Bible and Brain Science

You GOT THIS, Dad

AARON E. SHARP

HARVEST HOUSE PUBLISHERS
EUGENE, OREGON

Cover design by Bryce Williamson

Cover photos © slalomp, Nikunj Umretiya, Micko17, lushik / Getty Images

Published in association with Books & Such Literary Management, 52 Mission Circle, Suite 122, PMB 170, Santa Rosa, CA 95409-5370, www.booksandsuch.com.

You Got This, Dad
Copyright © 2020 by Aaron E. Sharp
Published by Harvest House Publishers
Eugene, Oregon 97408
www.harvesthousepublishers.com

ISBN 978-0-7369-7831-6 (pbk.)
ISBN 978-0-7369-7832-3 (eBook)

Library of Congress Cataloging-in-Publication Data

Names: Sharp, Aaron (Aaron E.), author.
Title: You got this, dad / Aaron Sharp.
Description: Eugene, Oregon : Harvest House Publishers, [2020]
Identifiers: LCCN 2019028524 (print) | LCCN 2019028525 (ebook) | ISBN 9780736978316 (trade paperback) | ISBN 9780736978323 (ebook)
Subjects: LCSH: Fatherhood—Popular works. | Fathers—Life skills guides. | Pregnancy—Popular works. | Childbirth—Popular works.
Classification: LCC HQ756 .S4785 2020 (print) | LCC HQ756 (ebook) | DDC 306.874/2—dc23
LC record available at https://lccn.loc.gov/2019028524
LC ebook record available at https://lccn.loc.gov/2019028525

Printed in the United States of America

19 20 21 22 23 24 25 26 27 / BP-AR / 10 9 8 7 6 5 4 3 2 1

To MOM AND DAD

A book probably shouldn't begin with the writer admitting that he doesn't have the words for something. But trying to express my love and appreciation for the two of you has left me feeling as if I have a most inadequate grasp of the English language. I love God because you taught me to. I love books because you taught me to. Who and what I am today can be traced back to the two of you. Like the proverbial turtle on a fencepost, I know I did not get here by myself. No son was ever as blessed as this one.

PS If you don't like how you are portrayed in chapter 22, I would just like to remind you that the two of you have always encouraged me to pursue writing. So really, it's your own fault.

Don't you see that children are GOD's best gift?
the fruit of the womb his generous legacy?
Like a warrior's fistful of arrows
are the children of a vigorous youth.
Oh, how blessed are you parents,
with your quivers full of children!
Your enemies don't stand a chance against you;
you'll sweep them right off your doorstep.

PSALM 127:3-5 MSG

You should never say anything to a woman
that even remotely suggests you think she's
pregnant unless you can see an actual baby
emerging from her at that moment.

DAVE BARRY, *DAVE BARRY TURNS FIFTY*

CONTENTS

THE SHARP TEAM

As a sports fan, I am intimately familiar with the concept of a team's roster. The roster is a list of all the players on that team. Some of those players are starters, and some of them are reserves. But they all make up part of the team. If you don't happen to be a sports fan, don't worry. I promise to keep the athletic analogies to a minimum, but I thought it might be helpful for you to get to know the Sharp team before we get going.

THE STARTING LINEUP

Aaron Sharp (dad; author of this book). I play a lot of roles for team Sharp. I am the family muscle (not the brains). Once when my wife, Wonder Woman, was pregnant, I got put in charge of the family calendar, and we showed up to a going-away party a full week early. I play catch, lift ballerinas in dance parties, read bedtime stories, and grill steaks. My catchphrase is "Go back to bed." I am a founding member of team Sharp.

Wonder Woman (Elaina Sharp; wife of Aaron; mother of four small humans; editor and footnoter of this book). In our family, Wonder Woman is the brains to my brawn. She is what makes our family go. If it wasn't for her, none of us would know what we were doing, where we were supposed to be doing it, or when we were supposed to be doing it. The kids might end up at my job, and I might end up at preschool. Chaos would reign. She is a seamstress, an avid reader, and a writer. She works a full-time job, is in charge of the kids' educations, and generally puts up with shenanigans from the five other members of the team. She is without a doubt the team MVP. Throughout this book, her footnotes provide her perspective on my perspective of pregnancy. She is a founding member of team Sharp.

The Zoologist (firstborn small human; lover of all things animal). The Zoologist, like all firstborns, believes it falls to him to make the rules, most of which benefit him. As the firstborn, he has been on the receiving end of more of his father's parenting missteps than the other children (no doubt this will come up in counseling one day). As this was our first pregnancy, it was—as you will read in this book— full of adventure, wonder, and more than a little trepidation. For as long as anyone can remember, he has loved animals and has consistently stated that his life goal is to be an animal expert.

The Ballerina (second-born small human; lover of all things beautiful). The Ballerina was the first baby girl in our family, and she has brought a style all her own. She loves to dance, accessorize, and dress up as a princess. The Ballerina lives to perform. From her dance recitals to her killer chicken impersonation, she lights up when there is a chance to show off in front of a group. She also is the little mother of the other three Sharp kids. Sometimes this means she is compassionate, and sometimes it just means she wants to boss everyone around. This second pregnancy was when we first encountered bed rest, both at home and at the hospital. She was also our second NICU (neonatal intensive care unit) baby.

The Fashionista (third-born small human; lover of expressing her independence, primarily by making her own fashion choices). The Fashionista was easily the toughest baby of the Sharp bunch. For a while, I still thought the Zoologist was the toughest, but by the time we got to six months, I had to concede that the Fashionista had him beat. Even at a young age, the Fashionista knew what she wanted. If she wanted her paci, you had better get her a paci. As a baby in the bassinet, if she was crying and didn't want the paci, God help you if you tried to give her one. Pregnancy number three produced our second bed rest and our first child to avoid the NICU. Even then, she was doing it her way.

The Jedi (fourth-born small human; lover of anything that can be kicked, bounced, or thrown). The Jedi's birth brought balance to the Sharp family force. He also brought a love of life and adventure. I've heard that as you go farther down the birth order, children get less risk averse. While I was writing this book, the Jedi got to go to the emergency room for the first time. Then, a week later, he got to go again. I guess it is all part of being the youngest of four children. Pregnancy number four was relatively uneventful as Sharp family pregnancies go. There was no bed rest before the birth and no NICU after the birth, and we showed up for the induction hours early. The only real drama during this pregnancy—or more accurately, during his delivery—was caused by his siblings, but we will get to all that in time.

THE RESERVES

A good team will have a good starting lineup, but a great team will also have good reserves on the bench to pitch in when the starters are sick, fatigued, or just off their game. The Sharp team is blessed with a deep bench.

At points in this book, there will be occasional references to Opa and Mimi (my parents) or Pops and Nindee (Wonder Woman's parents). We are fortunate to have our parents and siblings near us. I have great respect for people who have children and raise them without any family nearby. On more than a few occasions during a pregnancy, we have sent out a desperate plea for help and were thankful to have family there to throw us a lifeline.

And now let's begin our journey by talking about positive pregnancy tests and finding out there's a baby on the way.

WE'RE HAVING A BABY!

If you're reading this book, you, someone you love, or possibly someone you are related to by marriage needs it. This is a book about a dad's perspective on the miracle of pregnancy and childbirth. This is not a how-to book. The list of things I could write a how-to book about is short, and God surely knows that parenting does not make that list.

> The list of things I could write a how-to book about is short, and God surely knows that parenting does not make that list.

PREGNANCY EXPERTISE

You may be reading this book hoping to find the wisdom of an expert. In my opinion, there are two kinds of experts in life.

The first kind of expert is a person like Bill Gates. Gates is currently one of the richest and most well-known people in the world. He started programming computers at the age of 13. He attended Harvard University only to drop out to cofound a software company we know today as Microsoft. If you use a computer, a smartphone, or really any piece of technology, there's a good chance it was influenced by him. He is an icon in the computing world. Bill Gates is a genuine expert in technology.

An example of the second kind of expert is Roy Sullivan. You probably haven't heard of him. He was a park ranger in Virginia's Shenandoah National Park. He was neither rich nor famous, though he did gain some notoriety when he made the *Guinness Book of World Records* in 1977. Sullivan's claim to fame? He was the only living man to be struck by lightning four times. But the lightning wasn't finished with Roy Sullivan. He was reportedly struck three more times in his life. Sullivan was not a meteorologist. He didn't create lightning, and he didn't know why it struck him so many times. Yet I would suggest that he was a lightning expert. Think about it. Who knows more about what it feels like to be struck by lightning than Roy Sullivan?

When it comes to a dad's perspective on pregnancy and infants, I'm the second kind of expert. It's not unusual for my prayers to start with "God, I'm not sure *how* this happened, but…" More often than I'd like to admit, I don't even know *what* happened. But I've survived four pregnancies, even if my hair is a little singed, I'm twitching, and my short-term memory is shot.

> **Finding out your wife is pregnant is one of the most amazing, wonderful, and surreal moments of your life. It can also be terrifying.**

PREGNANCY EMOTIONS

Finding out your wife is pregnant is one of the most amazing, wonderful, and surreal moments of your life. It can also be terrifying. If you aren't quaking in your boots, Nikes, Skechers, or whatever, that's probably because you don't know enough yet to fully appreciate what news like that means.

If you are a man who just discovered that your wife is pregnant and you are unsure how you should feel, here is a simple test:

Do you feel like you are at the top of a massive roller coaster that does loops, breaks the sound barrier, and is typically described as death-defying?

Are you also unsure if you are properly latched into your seat or if this ride somehow skirted past government regulations about safety harnesses?

If you answered yes to those questions, then your emotions are tracking well with dad-to-be syndrome.

If you feel supremely confident, well rested, and calm, then you are either naive or foolish, or maybe this is your first child. Or all of the above. Thank God for naivete. Right now, you are like Spider-Man just after he was bitten by a radioactive spider. You feel a little funny and think everything is okay, but you have no idea what's coming. You are about to be responsible for the life of another human being!

For some reason, an all-knowing, all-powerful God has sovereignly chosen you to be a parent, the most important job in the world.

If that doesn't make you nervous, then I don't think you understand the gravity of the situation. It can be tempting to think, "Well, I already take care of my wife," and maybe you do. Maybe you pay all the bills, clean the house, do all the laundry, and wash all the dishes. If that is your situation, then good for your wife. She is an incredibly blessed woman. (More likely, your wife does a great job taking care of you, but let's not get off topic.)

Your wife may depend on you for certain things,[1] but odds are if she had to, she could take care of herself. More than likely, she can take care of herself much better than you can. A baby will not be like that.

The baby is going to be completely, totally, 100 percent dependent on you. Yes, you—the guy who forgot to pay the cable bill last month, the guy who lost the grocery list and just bought a bunch of frozen pizzas, the guy who can't do a load of laundry without shrinking his wife's shirts.[2]

A small, helpless bundle of joy will soon look at you, expecting you to already possess the knowledge needed to take care of him or her. If you turn out to be completely inept, this poor kid doesn't have a chance. If your wife discovered that for your entire dating life, you managed to hide the fact that you are a pathetic loser, that is unfortunate for her, but she bears *some* responsibility for not having a better process for screening the candidates for her future husband.

ELAINA SHARP CHIMES IN

[1] Like holding my hair back when I'm tossing my cookies for the umpteenth time with morning sickness.

[2] All. The. Time. But can I really complain if he's helping with the laundry?

> This kid is stuck with you for better or worse...and didn't get a say in the matter.

But this child who will soon call you Dad didn't have the luxury of choice. This kid is stuck with you for better or worse…and didn't get a say in the matter.

So yeah, this is the part where you should be somewhere on the scale between anxious and falling to your knees crying, "Good Lord (and I mean that with all reverence), what have we done?"

The realization hits dads at different times. Some dads-to-be are fine until they're on the way to the hospital. Some are fine until they see their child for the first time. And some dads begin to lose their marbles the moment their wife says, "Honey, we're pregnant."

I'm going to be completely honest with you. I'm a veteran of four pregnancies, but I have no recollection when it first hit me that another human being was now reliant on me for everything. (Remember, the loss of short-term memory is a common casualty of parenting.) I only remember one of the four times Wonder Woman told me we were pregnant. I remember lots of pregnancy tests, which are among the strangest parts of this whole operation.

PREGNANCY TESTS

> In this age of technology, the best method we have for detecting a new life growing in a woman is by her urinating on a stick.

In this age of technology, the best method we have for detecting a new life growing in a woman is by her urinating on a stick. I'm sure there is some fancy science involved in all of this, but it does feel a little like hocus-pocus.

At some point, the test comes back with two lines instead of one. Well, even this isn't as clear-cut as it may seem. Medical science has made great improvements in pregnancy tests in recent years, but with our first pregnancy, there was a lot of staring at the stick trying to decipher if there were two lines or not. If this is your first pregnancy, your wife probably spent hours peering at her freshly contaminated stick, trying to decipher if there was a second line or not. So if her depth perception seems off when she tells you that you are going to be a father, don't panic. It should clear up soon.

There is a good chance this whole bringing-a-new-life-into-the-world thing has hit your wife a lot faster and harder than it will hit you. In a very scientific poll, 100 percent of the men I interviewed in the mirror confirmed this is the case.

A woman's pregnancy is initially very conceptual to her husband. One minute you are lying in bed as a dude who is a husband. The next moment your wife is jumping up and down on the bed telling you that you are now a husband *and* a father. Nothing in your everyday life has changed—yet. For your wife, everything has already changed. Things are happening inside of her, so she feels pregnant. You just feel tired and a little disoriented because she woke you out of a deep sleep to share the news.

Then again, you may find out that you are going to be a father (or a father again) in a Chick-fil-A.

Wonder Woman tells me this is how things went down with baby number three.[3] It's important to note that baby number three didn't sleep for the first eight months of her life, so there's a good chunk of this period of time I don't recall. It's like I got the mother of all concussions and part of my memory is just a blank recording. Dead air.

> The human body's inability to remember if it is sleep deprived is a gift from God. Without that gift, no one would have more than one child, and the human species would slowly die out.

The human body's inability to remember if it is sleep deprived is a gift from God. Without that gift, no one would have more than one child, and the human

---

ELAINA SHARP CHIMES IN
[3] I told him about baby number four in Chick-fil-A. I can't believe he can't keep them all straight.

species would slowly die out. There are aspects of pregnancy I intend to ask God about one day. Sleep deprivation is high on the list.

It is important to note you can respond in various ways when you learn your wife is pregnant. It often depends on what number child this is. If this is your first go-round at being a father, you are a blank slate. The wonder of the moment numbs you to the shock of what's going on. If this isn't your first child, your mind probably fast-forwards to concepts like deductibles and available vacation time. If this is your wife's fourth (or more!) baby on the way, what loops through your mind is the scene from the Lord of the Rings movie *The Two Towers* right before the major battle at Helm's Deep when King Théoden, King of Rohan, surveys the massive attacking army and says, "So it begins."[4]

Which brings us to our next topic: pregnancy, hormones, and fastballs.

ELAINA SHARP CHIMES IN
[4] More like "So it continues."

HOW HORMONES ARE LIKE FASTBALLS...AND OTHER NECESSARY PIECES OF ADVICE

A few months into Wonder Woman's fourth pregnancy, I watched a fascinating baseball documentary named *Fastball*. These two events may seem completely unrelated. At first, I didn't see the connection either, but a clear parallel exists between the two.

Early in pregnancy number four, my wife and I had what was easily the worst argument of our marriage.[1] We'd been married almost a dozen years, and big arguments were pretty rare. The argument was tear-producing. It was actually the reason we told the other three kiddos Mommy was pregnant. I had to either say, "Listen, kids, Dad really blew it and was a jerk to your mom," or I had to say, "Hey, kids, Mommy is crying because she has a baby in her tummy." I chose the latter. Don't judge.

> I had to either say, "Listen, kids, Dad really blew it and was a jerk to your mom," or I had to say, "Hey, kids, Mommy is crying because she has a baby in her tummy." I chose the latter. Don't judge.

ELAINA SHARP CHIMES IN

[1] I don't even remember what this massive argument was about. Five dollars says neither does Aaron.

21

Shortly after this argument, I had an epiphany about the relationship between the 100-mph fastball and pregnancy hormones. I'm not going to claim this idea is divinely inspired, but you might conclude that there is some providence at work.

BASEBALLS HIGH AND TIGHT

The documentary was fascinating for many reasons. Among the many players interviewed were a handful of high-caliber hitters, several of whom were in baseball's hall of fame. Almost to a man, they emphatically claimed that a 100-mph fastball is often rising as it crosses the plate.

That didn't seem totally crazy until they interviewed physicists who explained that it is physically impossible. A baseball is pitched at a downward angle, and no matter how hard you throw it as it approaches the plate, it is losing speed and its height is dropping. Without some outside force acting on it, baseballs flying through the air don't suddenly start rising when they were headed downward.

So either God is working a miracle outside of the laws of physics on every baseball thrown that fast or baseballs headed down don't suddenly go up. I'll not say dogmatically that the Almighty isn't doing this, because He hasn't specifically mentioned it in the Bible, but I think we should probably look for another explanation.

Here is where brain science gets fascinating. No denying, 108 mph is fast. That's as fast as Baptists leave a room when there is dancing involved.[2] A fastball traveling at that speed reaches home plate in 396 milliseconds. Incidentally, this is also roughly the same amount of time it takes our four kids to transform a room from clean to chaos.[3] What 396 milliseconds means is that a batter can't watch the ball from the time it leaves the pitcher's hand until it crosses the plate. Essentially, a batter sees the ball in the pitcher's hand, and then he looks at the plate. Because they can't watch the trajectory of the ball the whole way, the batter's brain fills in the gap with what you might think of as a flight plan. The ball's path between the pitcher's mound and home plate is a result of the batter's brain making calculations and assumptions based on available information.

ELAINA SHARP CHIMES IN

[2] Hey, I grew up Baptist, and we enjoyed plenty of great "foot functions."

[3] It's cute when he underestimates our kids. I've seen them tear the place apart in half that time.

The problem facing a batter is that a fastball traveling at more than 100 mph has such speed and backspin that it doesn't drop at the rate of a slower fastball of, say, 92 mph. As a result, the ball is dropping at a different rate and angle than the brain anticipated. This means that the flight plan the brain filed for the path of the baseball located it lower than it was in reality. When the ball comes in higher than the brain said it would, the batter "sees" it as if it is rising. A ball thrown that fast can function as an optical illusion to a batter.

You might be wondering how this relates to pregnancy hormones, and I'm getting to that. Living through four pregnancies makes me a wily veteran of husbanding while pregnant, at least in this century. Susanna Wesley, who was the youngest of 25 children and gave birth to 19 children herself, would view me as a rank amateur. In the twenty-first century, however, having four children is often viewed as strange, self-destructive behavior. The two biggest reactions I get are "On purpose?" and "Do you know why that keeps happening?"

So as husbands go, I am the equivalent of an elder statesman.

HORMONE CHIN MUSIC

The whole process of what happens to a woman's body during pregnancy is amazing. God absolutely knew what He was doing when He decided women would bear children rather than men. I'm a dreadful person to be around when I have a headache. Yet somehow my lovely wife manages to operate at a high level while all of this is going on in her body. I know that Genesis tells us Eve was formed from Adam's rib. But I have to think God also included some other divine substance, because pregnancy makes it clear that men and women are made of different materials.

> I know that Genesis tells us Eve was formed from Adam's rib. But I have to think God also included some other divine substance, because pregnancy makes it clear that men and women are made of different materials.

What sadly took me four pregnancies to realize is that pregnancy hormones are to a marital relationship what a 100-mph fastball is to a baseball player's batting average. When Wonder Woman and I had a lengthy and animated discussion at the beginning of our most recent pregnancy, I was woefully unprepared for the change pregnancy hormones were making in how we interacted. You might be thinking, "Hadn't he figured some of this out already?" No, no, I had not. Which isn't that astounding since one of the challenges of pregnancy is that hormones often take the women experiencing them by surprise too.[4]

First Peter 3:7 (ESV) instructs husbands to "live with your wives in an understanding way," which is a challenge under normal circumstances. When a woman is pregnant, you are trying to live with "understanding" with someone who doesn't even understand herself. Husbands can be forgiven for feeling like Peter should have included a pregnancy exemption.

What happens to couples who have been married for any length of time is that the brain files a flight plan for how any argument is going to go. You know what you tend to do, you know what your spouse tends to do, and so you navigate the issue, work things through, and come out the other side because of the predictability of understanding one another. Each of you knows the other person. If you are committed to working your problems out, you can usually tackle most issues. Ideally, the longer you're married, the better you are at honoring God and each other, even when you would like to rip out the other person's eyeballs.

This is how things work under normal circumstances. But pregnancy hormones create anything but normal circumstances.

Instead of reacting in a manner that is typical for her (think of it as a 92-mph fastball), a pregnant woman reacts by bringing the heat. You settle into the batter's box thinking you are prepared for what is about to happen, and the next thing you know, the ball is humming toward you at 103 mph, and you are pretty sure she is aiming for your head.[5]

This leads a man into uncharted territory. His brain says the pitch is going to be low and away, and instead it comes in high and tight. Suddenly a rather minor

---

ELAINA SHARP CHIMES IN

[4] Let the Pregnancy Brain Games begin!

[5] I would never! (Said with a completely innocent, wide-eyed expression.)

issue can leave a husband swinging and missing while wondering what has happened to his wife.

For us, a minor issue was that my pregnant better half started asking me questions while I was brushing my teeth.[6] Few things in life annoy me more than someone expecting me to talk while I have a mouthful of toothpaste. If I try to answer, I end up making a colossal mess, so I generally mumble "In a mimit" or just give a dirty look.

Usually Mrs. Sharp takes this quirk of mine in stride, but not when she is pregnant. When pregnant, she doesn't find my surliness funny or cute. She considers it infuriating. When she got irritated at my refusing to answer a question while I brushed my teeth, my brain filed a flight plan for how the next few minutes were going to go. My brain was wrong. I didn't realize it, but I was in the position Goliath was in just as David was releasing the stone.

The best-case scenario for any husband in this situation is to live to bat another day. Your wife is throwing a blazing fastball, and your goal isn't to get a base hit. It is to make it through the at-bat without taking one on the chin. Don't try to be a hero.

> Your wife is throwing a blazing fastball, and your goal isn't to get a base hit. It is to make it through the at-bat without taking one on the chin. Don't try to be a hero.

I've shared this analogy with a few guys, and generally everyone agrees that it makes sense. So at some point during pregnancy number four, I shared it with Wonder Woman's OB/GYN. She listened intently as I explained my theory as to how 100-mph fastballs and pregnancy hormones are alike. When I was finished theorizing, she proclaimed that not only was I onto something, but my theory applied to other times in a woman's life, such as menopause. She then proceeded to

---

ELAINA SHARP CHIMES IN

[6] Well look at that, he did remember. IOU $5, babe.

pull out her cell phone and call her husband so I could explain my now-expanded theory of fastballs and hormones to him.

He listened intently before assuring me he wasn't sure why his wife thought he needed to hear this. Their marriage was a perfect one, he said, but he felt he might be able to use this analogy when mentoring younger men, so he was glad I told him.

I guess swinging and missing isn't exclusive to dealing with pregnancies.

This brings us to morning sickness, which contrary to the name, isn't exclusive to mornings.

TIMES OF UPHEAVAL

If you bought this book on pregnancy, childbirth, and infancy and didn't anticipate the discussion of bodily functions that follows, I don't know what to tell you. This is the first chapter that will deal with such topics, but it will not be the last.

Pregnancy is not for the faint of heart. I'll do my best to deal with these topics with humor and wit, but if you absolutely can't handle discussions of projectile vomiting, painful bloating, awful gas, and other horrors experienced by dads, how are you ever going to handle the parts about what *mothers* endure?

This discussion of the you-know-whats will at least be more enjoyable than the bodily functions chapter in Leviticus (look it up), although it is certainly less inspired.

"MORNING" SICKNESS

> Calling what a woman undergoes during pregnancy "morning sickness" is like referring to a 15-car pileup on the interstate as a fender bender.

Calling what a woman undergoes during pregnancy "morning sickness" is like referring to a 15-car pileup on the interstate as a fender bender. When Wonder Woman was pregnant with our first child, she was sick. *The. Entire. Pregnancy.* She was sick in the morning. She was sick in the evening. She was sick in the middle of the night. She was sick at noon. She was sick during the fall, the winter, and the spring. The only reason she wasn't sick in the summer was that she wasn't pregnant in the summer.

The places where that poor woman got sick included, but were not limited to,

our master bath

our guest bath

our front yard

our backyard

along the side of the road

a Styrofoam cup in her car while driving in bumper-to-bumper traffic at rush hour[1]

the church bathroom

a gas station bathroom

the bathrooms of numerous restaurants

out the window while we were driving down the road[2]

the kitchen sink

the master bathroom sink

the guest bathroom sink

the bathroom at work

the other bathroom at work

trash cans of various shapes and sizes at multiple locations

> Anybody who tells you they know exactly why something goes on in one pregnancy but not another is probably making it up.

ELAINA SHARP CHIMES IN

[1] Also, plastic bags of every shape and size in the car.

[2] Nope, never.

I could go on, but you get the idea. For many pregnancies, there is nothing "morning" about morning sickness. Each of our four children affected their mother differently in the womb. My wife was more nauseated with the boys. I'm sure there is an old wives' tale about the gender of the child, or babies with a full head of hair, or some other silliness, but pregnancies are wildly unpredictable. Anybody who tells you they know exactly why something goes on in one pregnancy but not another is probably making it up. Pregnancy itself is the result of something we understand. But beyond that, you begin to realize why the word "miraculous" is so easily attached to having children.

At some point during Wonder Woman's first pregnancy, I took to naming the nausea[3] and its effects "vomitous episodes." She threw up for nine months straight. The least I could do was come up with a funny term for the process. After conception, men have very little to do with the actual growth of a child inside a mother's womb, so we have to find other ways to contribute.

> After conception men have very little to do with the actual growth of a child inside a mother's womb, so we have to find other ways to contribute.

"REMEDIES"

As mentioned earlier, one thing you should be prepared for in pregnancy is the sudden appearance of "experts." Once people know you're going to be welcoming a new life into your home, they feel free to educate you about whatever their particular crusade is.

The "you must breastfeed children until they go to high school" people will corner you.

The "you must always let them cry it out or you'll raise a spoiled, entitled brat" people will make sure to load you down with literature.

Then there are the natural childbirth advocates, the essential oil believers, and

ELAINA SHARP CHIMES IN
[3] That's a rude nickname for your wife.

a host of other people all supporting their causes. You should be prepared for them in general (this issue will come up again later in the book), but know that when it comes to this chapter's topic, they all believe they have the answer for morning sickness.

If your wife is pregnant and one of these miracle home remedies works for you, congratulations. But if I were you, I would be careful mentioning the secret remedy to other pregnant women. Because if you get their hopes up (with raspberry tea, ginger tea, Vitamin B256 or whatever the number was, or rubbing Vicks on her feet—wait, that was for a head cold), when they are finally able to speak through their tears after throwing up yet again, they might forget it and want to forget you.

One of the strongly held beliefs about morning sickness is that ginger is an effective remedy for the vomitous episodes. (See, doesn't that just sound better than vomiting, puking, or upchucking?) With baby number one, I made a trip to the grocery store to get ginger ale in hopes it would help calm the nausea. It did absolutely nothing for my wife, but I personally found that my stomach settled down when I drank it.

Another suggestion was saltine crackers. For Wonder Woman, these usually came up as quickly as they went down, just like the ginger. Various other ideas include mint, sour candy, and herbal teas. Maybe those things work for other people, but that wasn't our experience. As I've said previously, this is yet another one of the ways we know that God is sovereign and in complete control of everything and has been since the beginning of time. Women endure things like this so much better than men.[4]

> If you told a man that he might be throwing up for nine months, he would eat nothing but cheeseburgers, pizza, ice cream, and pie the entire time.

Even with all the vomitous episodes, my wife was still taking her prenatal vitamins and trying to eat well for herself and the baby. If you told a man that he might

---

ELAINA SHARP CHIMES IN
[4] Yup.

be throwing up for nine months, he would eat nothing but cheeseburgers, pizza, ice cream, and pie the entire time. Why not, if you are just going to throw it all up anyway? That's like minus calories. Might as well enjoy at least the first part of the process.

MORNING SICKNESS—WHAT YOU CAN DO

Looking back over this chapter, I realize it might leave a soon-to-be dad or mom feeling down and discouraged, which was not my intent at all. The good news is that even the worst morning sickness usually stops with childbirth. Perhaps it would be best to end this chapter with some words of practical encouragement and hints to help you get through the vomitous episodes, whether they last for a trimester, or two, or even three. Consider these Aaron's morning sickness proverbs. I am fairly certain that were Solomon alive today, he would agree.

First, purchase as many buckets as you can afford. Place them around the house in strategic locations. I would suggest that a pregnant woman never be more than 36 inches away from a bucket regardless of whether that may seem practical. And consider brightly colored buckets to make the experience more aesthetically pleasing. (Forget that last sentence. My female agent suggested I add that.)

Second, if this isn't your first pregnancy, be prepared for older siblings to walk up to buckets and mimic their mom throwing up in them. When our first son, who was two at the time, pulled this stunt, I considered it one of the funniest things I have ever seen. It made his mom nauseous.[5]

Third, when someone tells you of the magic cure for morning sickness, give them a nice warm smile, but keep the expectations low—very low. A good rule of thumb is to only truly care about advice if it is coming from someone willing to babysit the child after it is born. Those people are invested in the process. Other people are just telling you what they read on the internet.

ELAINA SHARP CHIMES IN

[5] It was especially "hilarious" when he was mimicking me *while* I was throwing up. In the same bucket. Do you know how hard it is to avoid throwing up on your child while he's making fun of you throwing up?

> **A good rule of thumb is to only truly care about advice if it is coming from someone willing to babysit the child after it is born. Those people are invested in the process.**

Fourth, if this is your third or fourth pregnancy and your kids are still young, be prepared for lots of anxiety and worry when Mommy has a vomitous episode. Also, and this is specifically for pregnant women, if this is baby number four, you need to understand one of the major differences in your life now. In your first pregnancy, your husband probably ran to your side every time you got sick.[6] He did this because he loved you and because he could. In pregnancy number four, when you get sick, your husband probably has his hands full with a three-ring circus in the other room. Now instead of running to your side, he pauses for a moment to send prayers and well wishes your way while trying to break up a food fight. It isn't personal. He still loves you very much, but circumstances have changed. He will check on you as soon as he scrapes the spaghetti off the ceiling.

Speaking of circumstances changing, this brings us to the topic of a man accompanying his wife to OB/GYN appointments.

ELAINA SHARP CHIMES IN

[6] He really was great at getting me washcloths and tissues and holding my hair back. The couple that vomits together stays together.

GOING TO THE OB/GYN

A trip to the OB/GYN office with your pregnant wife is a rite of passage for a father-to-be. A man's first trip to his wife's OB/GYN is a reasonably awkward situation,[1] but pregnancy is full of awkward situations, so you might as well get used to it. What should a guy know before his first visit into this uncharted territory?

> A man's first trip to his wife's OB/GYN is a reasonably awkward situation, but pregnancy is full of awkward situations, so you might as well get used to it.

THE BASICS

It is important to note that OB/GYN stands for "obstetrics" (things related to having a baby) and "gynecology" (the study of womanly stuff) as opposed to, say, "Off-Base and Gross, You kNow." Okay, it isn't all that important to know this. No one will ever ask you if you know what OB/GYN stands for, but when you accompany your wife to pregnancy appointments, you are going to be way, way, way out of your element. At least knowing the meaning of the acronym OB/GYN gives you one thing to feel good about.

ELAINA SHARP CHIMES IN

[1] Insert eye roll here. The one not in the stirrups feels awkward?

THE WAITING ROOM

Armed with the knowledge of what the acronym stands for, you can now confidently step into the OB/GYN waiting room. The second you enter, you'll glance around the room and a little voice in your head will say, "I don't think I'm supposed to be here." Ignore this voice. It is too late. There is no backing out now.

Three types of human beings will occupy the waiting room:

- women
- men accompanying their pregnant wives
- babies and small children accompanying their mom and/or parents

The women all seem relatively at home here. This is their doctor. Going to the OB/GYN is something mothers pass down to their daughters like family heirlooms, right? The babies and small children only know that they are in a waiting room where there aren't any snacks, juice, or cartoons unless their parents planned ahead. The way children act in the OB/GYN waiting room would be effective birth control if it wasn't too late already for most of the other people.

By baby number four, we were either finding a way to ship the kids off with their grandparents or rolling into that office loaded with crackers, applesauce pouches, sippy cups, iPads, coloring books, and anything else that promised to occupy a child's attention. If a live rattlesnake would have kept them quiet, I would have considered it. Actually, that is a lie. I hate snakes.

The best part about the OB/GYN waiting room is, without a doubt, sizing up the other dudes in the waiting room. You can always spot a guy who's there with his wife for her first pregnancy. His eyes are as big as softballs, and he constantly looks around the room, trying to pretend he's not looking around the room.[2] He sticks as close to his wife as possible because he's afraid that if a distance of more than 13 inches opens up between them, someone might not know they are together, and then the guy just looks like a creep who's in the wrong room.

ELAINA SHARP CHIMES IN
[2] The impish part of me may or may not have delighted a bit in their awkwardness.

In short, when it's a man's first go-round at the OB/GYN, he tends to be nervous about the waiting room because he does not belong there—and everyone knows it.

In short, when it's a man's first go-round at the OB/GYN, he tends to be nervous about the waiting room because he does not belong there—and everyone knows it. If you've ever gotten mixed up and accidentally opened the door to the women's restroom, or perhaps even stepped in before realizing your mistake and hastily retreating, the OB/GYN provides a little bit of the same feeling. The difference is that you can't just turn around and run out hoping no one saw what you did. The same sensation is unmistakable: "I have trespassed. I have intruded on feminine territory and am probably about to be taken down by pepper spray or a Taser."

Any man worth his salt will play it cool, but as someone who has had multiple colonoscopies and a hernia surgery, I will tell you that my first trip to the OB/GYN was the most uncomfortable I have ever felt in a doctor's waiting room. This changes with more children. Eventually my nerves calmed and I was a veteran of the experience. By baby number three, I no longer felt like an intruder. Now I strode into the waiting room, greeted the receptionist, joked with the nurses about whether they needed a urine sample from me too, chitchatted with the doctor (who knew me by name), and even assisted in a couple of C-sections. Okay, I didn't assist in any C-sections, since that would be a HIPAA violation, but once you've accompanied your wife to the OB/GYN's office a couple dozen times, the waiting room is no longer a shrinking torture chamber.[3]

Now I strode into the waiting room, greeted the receptionist, joked with the nurses about whether they needed a urine sample from me too, chitchatted with the doctor (who knew me by name), and even assisted in a couple of C-sections.

ELAINA SHARP CHIMES IN

[3] You truly were one of the favorite husbands up there. Way to go, baby!

THE DOCTOR

I can't speak to all OB/GYNs everywhere; I really only know one. Since OB/GYNs are doctors and doctors are people, I assume they are pretty much like everyone else. There are good electricians and bad electricians. Flight attendants who are kind and others who drink a big cup of rude before stepping into the plane. Attorneys who are very knowledgeable and others who hope no one notices they haven't got a clue. My comments on OB/GYNs should be viewed in light of the smallest of sample sizes.

By the time of our first pregnancy, my wife had been going to her OB/GYN for a solid decade and a half. That's a good chunk of time, and it is pretty funny to think that my wife's OB/GYN has known my wife longer than I have. I don't think there is anything comparable for men. A man's doctor is personal, but not anywhere near this level. Maybe some guys have that type of a relationship with their barber or mechanic, but those are pretty rare.

We were very fortunate to have the OB/GYN we did because, and I'm going to let you in on a little secret here, pregnancies are hard.[4]

When we first started trying to get pregnant, I didn't know what to expect. Well, I knew how babies were made, but I was clueless about how the rest of the process worked. We spent six months trying to get pregnant, and then just at the time I was laid off from my job, we suffered a miscarriage.

It was an incredibly tough time in our lives. Six months later, I was still unemployed, and the pregnancy test showed positive—but there were complications. My wife's lab numbers were not going up as fast as they should have, and she was experiencing physical symptoms that were not positive indicators. I remember vividly a late-evening phone call between my wife and her doctor in which we were told that if the symptoms continued, we'd need to come in the next day. The doctor told us very clearly that most of the time, a woman who experienced these symptoms lost the pregnancy.

We hung up the phone and hoped the symptoms would get better, but instead they continued. After a long and restless night, we called the doctor's office and

---

ELAINA SHARP CHIMES IN

[4] Don't scare them away! Pregnancies are beautiful, it's all worth it in the end, blah blah blah.

made an appointment. We headed to the office, preemptively bracing ourselves for bad news while still praying for the best. At the time, and even thinking about it now, it all seems to have happened in slow motion—the drive to the hospital, the elevator ride to the office, sitting in the waiting room, and walking slowly back to the ultrasound room. If you've ever been in a similar situation, you'll understand the heaviness that hangs over everything. I hesitate to refer to these feelings as impending doom because it seems a touch dramatic, but they form a very odd mixture of hope, prayer, and what counselors call "anticipatory grief" as you try to mentally steel yourself for the bad news that you may be moments away from hearing.

This time, however, God had other plans.

As the sonogram began, we held hands and steadied ourselves to hear the silence that would signal another miscarriage. Instead, we were blown away by an active and healthy heartbeat, which to our ears sounded as loud as a football game halftime drumline.[5] We were the exceptions to the rule that the doctor had told us about. And here is where the OB/GYN really comes into play. My wife was fortunate to have a doctor who is a strong believer. I know that being a solid Christian does not make one a good doctor, but it is nice when you can have both.

That day, she came into the examination room and had her own little praise session over what God had done. The odds were against this pregnancy, but the Almighty and our little baby had other plans. I have always had a mental image of our little boy in the womb muttering to himself, "Progesterone? I don't need no stinkin' progesterone."

> For the rest of my life, the snapshot of our OB/GYN being so thankful and as blown away as we were at what God was doing in the miracle of childbirth will be one of my favorite pregnancy memories.

For the rest of my life, the snapshot of our OB/GYN being so thankful and as

ELAINA SHARP CHIMES IN

[5] I'm not crying; you're crying!

blown away as we were at what God was doing in the miracle of childbirth will be one of my favorite pregnancy memories.

But that doesn't mean I'm going back to the OB/GYN's office anytime soon. Especially not without my wife.

You may deal with the OB/GYN well, but this brings us to something else husbands handle with trepidation—the supersniffer.

THE SUPERSNIFFER

A significant amount of research exists suggesting that pregnancy does not affect a woman's sense of smell. Scientific journals, medical reviews, and well-respected magazines have all weighed in to debunk the idea that pregnant women have a heightened sense of smell. The mountain of evidence put forth by these studies is quite convincing.

And it is completely, totally, absolutely, without a doubt wrong.[1]

I'm sure the people who wrote these journal articles were well-educated professionals using excellent research methods. I am also confident none of them were pregnant, married to someone who is pregnant, or living in the same house with a pregnant woman.

THE REALITY OF THE SUPERSNIFFER

Ordinarily I'd be the first person to say something like "You should believe the data over anecdotal evidence," but in this case, the anecdotes are mine, those of every woman I have ever spoken to about this, and those of every dude who has ever lived with a pregnant wife. Read the studies and journal articles if you want. Just know that when you point to an article in a magazine and explain to a pregnant woman—who is revulsed at the smell of a cheeseburger on a commercial on TV—that her sense of smell isn't any different now than it was before she

---

ELAINA SHARP CHIMES IN
[1] I knew I liked you.

was pregnant, there is a very good chance you are about to either eat a magazine, be slapped upside the head with said cheeseburger, or (in extreme circumstances) be sent to meet your Maker at the hands of a hungry and nauseated woman who is great with child. You will be standing at the pearly gates when Saint Peter asks what happened, and you're going to have to tell him that your pregnant wife just killed you with her bare hands because your hair smelled funny.

Trust me, keep the scientific findings to yourself.

Tell me all you want about how a woman's sense of smell is not impacted by pregnancy, but I remember heating up a frozen beef and broccoli meal in the microwave during our first pregnancy. How did she react? Well, the good news is she didn't threaten my life, but it was articulated to me very clearly that there were two things I needed to understand. First, I was never again to even so much as think about putting something like that in the microwave while she was pregnant. Second, if I wanted to eat what I was currently microwaving, I would need to do so outside of the house. I could eat it in my car, on the back porch, or in our neighborhood park, but the meal was offending my wife's olfactory sense and had to leave the house immediately.[2]

Obviously, I survived the evening. I took Mrs. Sharp's words to heart and chose to view this as an opportunity to allow the Holy Spirit to help me grow in grace and compassion. It had little to do with survival instincts, or at least that's what I tell myself.

This heightening of the sense of smell in a pregnant woman leads to what has come to be known around our house as the supersniffer. The supersniffer phenomenon is so obvious that with at least one of our pregnancies, I knew that my wife was pregnant before we had a positive pregnancy test because of how sensitive her sense of smell had become.

> As a man, the rule of thumb with all things pregnancy-related is to imagine the worst possible scenario and then multiply by a factor of five.

ELAINA SHARP CHIMES IN

[2] This seems quite reasonable to me.

So exactly how much is a woman's sense of smell impacted by pregnancy? As with everything else in pregnancy, this depends on the woman and on the affect the child she is carrying is having on her body. But as a man, the rule of thumb with all things pregnancy-related is to imagine the worst possible scenario and then multiply by a factor of five. To be safe, make it ten. With that in mind, here are five simple rules to follow if you share a home, office, or planet with a woman who has a bun in the oven.

SURVIVING THE SUPERSNIFFER

First, if you think a smell is pleasant, it will most likely cause the pregnant woman in your vicinity to instantly develop nausea and a headache and induce swelling in her feet. Ignore the voice in your head that seeks to understand this phenomenon. Listen to the voice in your head telling you to do everything in your power to eradicate the smell with all due haste.[3]

Second, if you believe that a smell is slightly off-putting or perhaps just a little unpleasant, it will most definitely induce nausea, headaches, swelling, twitching, and convulsions in the pregnant woman you are near. It is in your best interests to dispense of this smell with extreme prejudice. Remember how after David struck Goliath in the forehead with the smooth stone, he still cut off his head? Apply the same sense of thoroughness to keeping smelly things away from the pregnant woman in question.

Third, if the smell a pregnant woman finds revolting comes from you, do not take it personally.[4] If the woman is your wife, it is possible, though in no way certain, that sometime after the child is a year or two old, she will have completely forgotten about her revulsion to your odoriferous emanations. If at any point during this pregnancy your body becomes hot enough to produce a drop of sweat, plan on taking a shower or two. I suggest that after mowing the yard you burn your clothes in the backyard and use the hose to rinse off before you enter the house to take a shower.

ELAINA SHARP CHIMES IN

[3] Also, the voice in your head should be telling you to give her lots of foot rubs and neck rubs.

[4] I feel it very necessary to defend myself here and point out to your many readers that I never objected to your smell, pregnant or not!

> When it comes to dealing with the supersniffer, you are playing a game in which you can fumble, make turnovers, fall out of bounds, strike out, commit a foul, or double-fault, but you can never possibly score any points.

Fourth, realize you can do nothing to make this any better. Adjust accordingly. When it comes to dealing with the supersniffer, you are playing a game in which you can fumble, make turnovers, fall out of bounds, strike out, commit a foul, or double-fault, but you can never possibly score any points. What smelled good before pregnancy no longer smells good. What smelled good in the first trimester no longer smells good in the second trimester. What smelled good Tuesday no longer smells good Friday. What smelled good at 8:00 a.m. no longer smells good at 8:05 a.m. Eat in the car, in the garage, or on the porch if you must. Consider incinerating sweaty gym clothes rather than bringing them back in the house. If you and your supersniffing wife are going to coexist for nine months in this state, it will require all the resourcefulness and creativity you can muster.

Fifth, buy candles. What variety? All of them. If you buy every scent available, there is a good chance that at least once or twice she will find the smell pleasing. Also, don't be surprised if the one smell she fixates on is something a little strange, like antibacterial wipes or dishwashing detergent. If you see her sniffing something repeatedly and she has a smile on her face, pay close attention and just go with it. If necessary, pretend that antibacterial wipes are the greatest blessing God ever gave our noses. But if you want to come through unscathed, do not in any way insinuate that your wife is doing something strange or out of the ordinary.

The supersniffer, like many of the unintended byproducts of pregnancy, drives a pregnant woman as crazy as it does those who are trying not to assault her senses. For nine months, she will feel like her sense of smell is the victim of an all-out assault of a world trying to make her nauseated, queasy, and irritable. Which brings us to the topic of cravings and aversions.

CRAVINGS AND AVERSIONS

As a husband, I really had it good when it came to cravings and aversions.[1] I had always heard horror stories of husbands running to the store at 3:00 a.m. to buy pickles and ice cream or some other strange combination. When Wonder Woman was expecting the first time, I went to bed every night wondering if this would be the night I would be pushed out from under the covers and told not to come back until I had returned from the store with tuna fish and peanut butter. Thankfully, that day never came.

> When Wonder Woman was expecting the first time, I went to bed every night wondering if this would be the night I would be pushed out from under the covers and told not to come back until I had returned from the store with tuna fish and peanut butter.

AVERSIONS

Because the senses of smell and taste are so closely related, a pregnant woman's aversions are greatly influenced by the supersniffer. A food that does not smell good, or at least has offended a pregnant woman's sense of smell, will be

---

ELAINA SHARP CHIMES IN

[1] You're welcome, babe.

an aversion. But there are other foods that she will think sound great and smell great…and then she will put those foods in her mouth, and everything will suddenly change. Faster than you can say "How does that taste, honey?" a food can go from the good list to the bad list.

Smells are a big contributor to aversions, but they are by no means the only contributor. Along with smells, textures have a way of wreaking havoc on the appetite of a pregnant woman. For whatever reason, my wife found the texture of chicken to be abhorrent during her pregnancies. I suspect this was at least partially influenced by her desire for me to grill numerous steaks. The texture of a nice medium-well steak was perfectly acceptable. I assume this was due to my wife's body signaling to her that steak would help her avoid anemia, something that's a constant concern for pregnant women, and not a mere hunger for well-grilled steak.[2] Then again, I do grill a mean steak. Of course, all these things take place in the hormone-haunted subconscious of a woman who is doing the difficult work of growing another human being inside her, so who really knows what is going on? Well, of course God does, but outside of the Father, Son, and Holy Spirit, no one knows what is going on in a pregnancy.

> Outside of the Father, Son, and Holy Spirit, no one knows what is going on in a pregnancy.

CRAVINGS

When I said that I was lucky with the aversions and cravings, I was serious. For all four of our pregnancies, Wonder Woman had several cravings, but they were all easily fulfilled. I didn't have to drive to the next town, get out of bed in the middle of the night, or do any type of special preparations.

The most consistent craving my wife had with her pregnancies was avocado soup at one of our favorite Mexican food restaurants. I am not a fan of avocado

ELAINA SHARP CHIMES IN
[2] Yeah, sure, let's go with that.

soup, but making consistent stops for the avocado soup meant I was also picking up nachos, queso, and whatever else sounded good. This kind of craving I can fully support. At times like these, a man needs to remember that the Scriptures clearly teach that being a husband means sacrificing. It means loving your wife and giving yourself for her. And if this amazing woman needs you to go get Mexican food for dinner seemingly every night for nine months, you take this opportunity to apply God's Word to your life and love your wife well by bringing home the soup, queso, flautas, nachos, fajitas, churros, and whatever else she needs. It is clearly the Christlike thing to do.

One of the more challenging things about this aspect of pregnancy is that everything changes from one pregnancy to another. In our area, there are several locations of a regionally well-known taco joint. It has been featured on the Food Network, and we both like it, although I have a greater affinity for these tacos than my wife does. And I know what you're thinking: "Those people eat a lot of Mexican food." Well, we live in Texas, and that's sort of par for the course. As comedian Jim Gaffigan said in an interview with an Austin newspaper, "If you go to Texas, there's authentically amazing barbecue, there's authentically amazing Mexican or Tex-Mex, and as you mentioned, steak is a big thing. So, there is a bit of a crisis that ensues when I'm going to Texas."[3,4] We Texans love our food almost as much as we love our football, and barbecue doesn't give you a concussion.

> We Texans love our food almost as much as we love our football, and barbecue doesn't give you a concussion.

We eat a lot of Mexican food, but that isn't the point. What is the point? The point is that this taco place is so good that it's nationally recognized. It makes national lists of best taco restaurants. Our house is about 35 minutes from the

---

ELAINA SHARP CHIMES IN

[3] Russ Espinoza, "Head over Meals," *Austin Chronicle*, October 17, 2014, https://www .austinchronicle.com/arts/2014-10-17/head-over-meals/.

[4] Hey, you're infringing on my footnote territory. Back off, man!

OB/GYN's office, and there happen to be two locations of this restaurant on the way, one of which is right around the corner from the hospital. During pregnancy number three, we got in the habit of going there after every doctor's visit. Every time we left the doctor's office, I would mention those tacos, and my wife would say, "Oh, that sounds good. Let's go there." It was a glorious nine months of taco eating.[5]

When we got pregnant with baby number four, I thought for sure I was about to spend nine months regularly visiting taco heaven, but it was not to be. After our first doctor's visit, I brought up this taco place again, thinking surely we would resume our post-doctor's-appointment tradition from the last pregnancy, only to have my wife say, "You know, that doesn't sound too good. Can we go somewhere else?" I had hoped this would be just a one-time thing, but as it turned out, not one time during the fourth pregnancy did those tacos sound good to my wife. Given that she was growing another human being inside her body while working, being a mom to three children, and everything else that goes into living everyday life, I again found myself needing to sacrifice. For pregnancy number four, I made sure to eat there regularly on my lunch break from work.

Since we are (loosely) on the topic of things that are ingested by pregnant women, it's probably as good a time as any to discuss the many and varied tests a pregnant woman must endure over the course of nine months. There will be blood tests, urine tests, and everyone's favorite—the glucose test. The glucose test occurs a little past halfway through the pregnancy, and its purpose is to check for gestational diabetes. This test involves fasting and then drinking a half a cup of a liquid that contains glucose. If you've ever had a colonoscopy, it is a similar experience, except the expectant mom is carrying a small human the size of a cantaloupe in her belly, and someone who is always hungry will be fasting for at least eight hours prior to the test. I have yet to meet anyone who thinks of or describes the glucose testing part of pregnancy as pleasant. This goes for men and women.[6]

ELAINA SHARP CHIMES IN

[5] You can thank me later. Or not, since that's how we got in the mess in the first place.

[6] Fact check: You don't have to fast for the first glucose test. But if you fail that first glucose test, you must do the longer, more tortuous glucose test that includes fasting.

> I have yet to meet anyone who thinks of or describes the glucose testing part of pregnancy as pleasant. This goes for men and women.

Just know that if she has a craving or just wants to eat or drink particular things while she is pregnant, it is a husband's job to have an ample supply of those things ready after the glucose test. Also, while she is fasting, it would be a good idea for you either not to eat or, at the very least, not to eat in front of your wife. If you feel you must partake of food during this time, it would be best to do so somewhere that the expectant mom cannot see you eating or smell the food. Also, don't advertise the fact that you ate. Certainly don't mention if you ate something she likes.

If you heed my words, you will see that even if you have to deal with some quirky behavior, perhaps even in the middle of the night, this is one part of pregnancy that can work out well for you.

It is possible that so far in this book I have really played up the stressful and tension-filled parts of pregnancy without mentioning the fun and endearing moments. There are many of these, but I would be remiss if I didn't point out that as a guy, being married to a pregnant woman essentially means giving her a blank check for just about anything she wants in life. Who turns down requests by pregnant women? Nobody. Well, at least not twice.

> I would be remiss if I didn't point out that as a guy, being married to a pregnant woman essentially means giving her a blank check for just about anything she wants in life.

Over the course of our pregnancies, I used the excuse "My wife is pregnant" to...

Get out of an international work trip. I didn't want to go, and the fact that my wife was pregnant was the perfect reason to stay home. Come to think of it, I did this several times at that job. My employer threatened to send me on a particular trip every two years, and we just kept having kids every two years, so I didn't have to go. If I was still working there, we might be up to six kids by now.[7] It actually became a running joke that we had kids every two years just so I could avoid that trip. Everyone laughed, but I don't think people knew for sure that wasn't what we were doing.

Ask for anything we wanted at a restaurant. You can ask for anything to be added or cut on a meal at pretty much any restaurant by saying, "My wife is pregnant, and she likes it this way." People in the food industry deal with pregnant women enough to know what's up. If the person taking your order is a woman who has been pregnant, you might even get part of the order for free. I've gone into a restaurant and basically asked for a bucket of ranch to be added to the order, and when the person taking the order gave me a strange look, I just told them my wife was pregnant. A look of understanding (and possibly compassion) crossed their face, and they just took care of it.

> If you are somewhere and you want to leave, having a pregnant wife is like having a Get Out of Jail Free card in Monopoly.

Leave early from a social engagement I didn't really want to go to anyway. I'm not saying we did this, and I'm not saying we didn't. All I'm saying is if you are somewhere and you want to leave, having a pregnant wife is like having a Get Out of Jail Free card in Monopoly. No one in their right mind is going to question this. The flip side is that having a pregnant wife will also mean you will leave early from a social engagement that you really want to be at. You can't have it both ways.

Refuse to move to the center of the pew in church. Choose to believe I am a bad church member if you want, but at times I just want to sit next to the aisle. Don't deny it; we've all been there. Well, if you have a pregnant wife and the usher asks you to move to the center of the pew, you have two approaches. You can try to handle this quietly by slyly pointing to your wife's belly. The problem with this is he might not get it. In this case, you will have to escalate things and point out to the

---

ELAINA SHARP CHIMES IN

[7] That's not funny.

usher that your wife is pregnant, will need to leave to go to the restroom approximately every 12 minutes during the service, needs the legroom…and if he makes her move to the center of the aisle, he might have heard his last sermon on this side of the pearly gates. At this point, he will generally be fine with you staying next to the aisle. You may also get a new usher by the time they pass the offering plates.

Don't fear the cravings and aversions. Lean into them. Embrace them. Start seeing these cravings and aversions for what they are—a brilliant opportunity. You will have bigger problems, which brings us to the topic of getting a good night's sleep while sharing a bed with a pregnant woman.

SHARING A BED WITH A PREGNANT LADY

A married couple's sleeping arrangements can be more than a little controversial before pregnancy is even part of the picture. A king-size bed is 72 inches (6 feet) wide. The approximate split between a husband and wife is 50 inches for the wife and 22 inches for the husband.[1] A queen-size bed is 60 inches wide, meaning that the husband has only 10 inches of space.

> If you are married and the two of you are sleeping on a bed smaller than a queen, then I have no idea how you are making it through the night without someone getting concussed. God bless you.

Wonder Woman and I invested in a king-size bed early in our marriage, but occasionally we sleep on a smaller bed in a hotel or while visiting someone. When this happens and we both suddenly realize we are about to spend the night with less than the 72 inches to which we have grown accustomed, we both think the same thing: "Uh-oh. Somebody's probably getting hurt tonight." And usually they do, but almost every time it is an accident. If you are married and the two of you are sleeping on a bed smaller than a queen, then I have no idea how you are making it through the night without someone getting concussed. God bless you.

ELAINA SHARP CHIMES IN

[1] I would scoff and roll my eyes here, but let's all just be honest and admit he is right. Whatevs.

If you are a man who is married to a pregnant woman sleeping on a smaller bed, I have to assume there is a special crown in heaven just for you.[2] I'm pretty sure this was something the apostle Paul wrote about at length in his third epistle to the Corinthians.

I can't speak for every marriage, but after comparing notes with other married couples, I feel confident that this struggle for mattress real estate is quite common. When a woman is pregnant, however, all previous arrangements are considered null and void. (As a side note, this principle applies to everything, not just sleeping arrangements. The sooner a man makes his peace with this concept, the smoother a lot of the pregnancy will go for him.) A husband who has learned to be content with his 22 inches will soon find that once his wife is pregnant, his slice of the mattress will dwindle throughout the pregnancy. There are a couple of reasons for this change.

THE PILLOWS COMETH

The average pregnant woman sleeps with 5.7 pillows. There is hard data to support this; I think I saw it on the internet. The average pregnant woman sleeps with every pillow in the house that is not under someone's head, and occasionally she will even requisition those if the ~~demon seed~~ miracle of life she is carrying in her tummy deems it necessary.

All of this is before the pregnant woman looks at her husband and informs him that it is time to purchase a pregnancy pillow. There are different types of pregnancy pillows. One of the most popular, which my great-with-child wife purchased, is large and U-shaped. As a husband, your first reaction will of course be relief. Your wife, who is having a devil of a time getting comfortable at night, will rest a little easier. You think this way because you are a good husband. Whatever you do, you naive man, never change—but don't be a fool. There will come a point after the implementation of said pillow that you realize the real estate for the pillow is going to come at the expense of your ever-shrinking 22 inches.

ELAINA SHARP CHIMES IN

[2] Or that said man has rightfully given over the queen bed to his glowing wife and has taken up residence on the couch, floor, guest bed, bathtub, or what have you.

I hope you are starting to catch on to the theme here, but this is a sacrifice you can and will be happy to make. If you are not happy to make it, there is a very good chance you will have the opportunity to assemble your own prayer chamber on the couch to consider the error of your ways.

> You can accommodate your pregnant wife and grow closer to God through prayer, or you can criticize your pregnant wife and likely soon find yourself in God's direct presence. Life is frequently about the choices we make. Choose wisely.

Speaking of prayer, when you are tempted to comment on this turn of events and possibly offer some constructive criticism, I suggest you turn to prayer. Pray for your wife. Pray for your unborn child. Pray for every person you know. Pray for every church you know. Pray for all the animals that you can think of. Pray until you fall asleep if you must, but keep your ideas to yourself. You have two options here, both of which involve you getting closer to God. You can accommodate your pregnant wife and grow closer to God through prayer, or you can criticize your pregnant wife and likely soon find yourself in God's direct presence. Life is frequently about the choices we make. Choose wisely.

THE DREAMS

If a pregnant woman's dreams are any indication, her subconscious must be a wild place. The hormones, the stress, and the anxiety inherent in childbirth combine to produce dreams that are as vivid as they are wacky.

As a newly married husband, I often found myself caught up in the adventures that were my wife's dreams. Her dreams tend to be very real, they can be influenced by what she just watched on TV, and they just might include me having to wake up to deal with them. On one occasion, we went to bed after having watched several hours of the TV show *24*. In the middle of the night, my lovely, sleeping wife rolled over and asked me if I had my Secret Service papers. By this time in our marriage, I had learned to know that even though she was asleep, if

I did not play along, her feelings would be hurt (in her sleep!).[3] Being the good husband that I am, I told her my papers were all in order. She rolled over satisfied that our bedroom was properly secured. I rolled over laughing. She hadn't even bothered to check my papers.

The Secret Service dream was par for the course before pregnancy, but after pregnancy things took a much more dramatic turn. For nine months, my wife's nightly sleep was filled with one strange episode after another. She talked about anything and everything in her sleep. Periodically she would get up in the middle of the night, get dressed, and climb back in bed. Lights were turned on at all hours of the night, which happens to be quality preparation for parenting small children. From time to time, she woke up angry at me for something I had done in her dreams. Apparently, the Aaron who inhabits my wife's subconscious can be a real jerk. I'm sure this has some great psychological meaning, but I'm choosing to leave it alone. The waking world is full of enough trouble; there's no use looking for more in the subconscious.

THE DISCOMFORT

Pregnant women are uncomfortable 100 percent of the time. Actually, that's probably a low estimate. If you doubt this, ask any pregnant woman. It's true. From pretty much the moment of conception, it is impossible for her to get comfortable. This goes for almost every facet of life, but it is the most pronounced when she is lying down in bed—when she really and truly wants and needs to be comfortable.

Over the course of nine months, a woman will sleep, or at least attempt to sleep, in every possible position imaginable. She will elevate, twist, and contort, but she will be fighting a losing battle. At some point, out of desperation, she might try sleeping on the couch. This will not work, but the closer she gets to her due date, the more willing she is to try anything. On more than a few occasions while my wife was pregnant, I was sure we were about to buy sleeping bags that attach to the wall, like they have on the space shuttle. If it would have worked, she would have tried it. I never encouraged this idea because the odds of me ending up in one of

---

ELAINA SHARP CHIMES IN

[3] You say that as if it were not perfectly understandable.

those sleeping bags after once again having said something insensitive would have been quite high.

YOU

> At some point in every pregnancy, the woman looks at her husband and says the five words that have been on her mind since she first began feeling the effects of growing another human being inside her: "You did this to me."

One other factor contributes to a pregnant woman's sleep difficulties—her husband. You—yes, you—are no doubt cramping your pregnant wife's sleeping style. Whether it is your perpetual snoring, your stubborn insistence on occupying more than 22 inches of the mattress, or just the infuriating way you are unconscious the moment your head hits the pillow,[4] you need to understand you are part of the problem. At some point in every pregnancy, the woman looks at her husband and says the five words that have been on her mind since she first began feeling the effects of growing another human being inside her: "You did this to me." Keep it in mind when you go to bed at night. Odds are you will sleep soundly while your poor saint of a wife is in agony.

So when, in the middle of the night, she kicks you harder than you have ever been kicked and says, "I had a cramp," don't challenge her story.[5] The look on her face may say, "No, that wasn't an accident. Go ahead, say something. You feeling lucky, punk?"

Just say, "It's okay, baby. I'm sorry you are having a cramp," and act like she didn't just break your femur, even if she did.

The average man knows very little about what happens during pregnancy. When his wife snarls at him and says "You did this to me" in her most accusatory tone, he doesn't really grasp the enormity of the situation, which brings us to birthing classes.

ELAINA SHARP CHIMES IN

[4] So. Annoying.

[5] I have no idea what you are talking about!

BIRTHING CLASSES

Almost all pregnancies have much in common. Visiting the OB/GYN, telling family members that you're expecting, sonograms, deciding on a name, packing for the hospital…these things and more happen with every pregnancy. Have enough kids and you can feel a little like Bill Murray in the movie *Groundhog Day*.

Other aspects of having a bun in the oven—such as morning sickness, aversions, cravings, and registering for baby showers—may or may not happen, or they may happen but in completely different ways. Then there are the things that happen only during a couple's first ride on the pregnancy merry-go-round. Thankfully, birthing classes are in this category.

> I was a reasonably intelligent person before I became a father. Now I am doing good to remember my children's names and put all my clothes on before I leave the house in the morning.

As I write this chapter, our firstborn, the Zoologist, is seven years old. Publishing a book is a long process, so by the time this book releases, about nine years will have passed since Wonder Woman and I attended our mandatory three birthing classes at the hospital where my wife would give birth. Nine years. That is almost a decade of dad brain. I was a reasonably intelligent person before I became a father.

Now I am doing good to remember my children's names and put all my clothes on before I leave the house in the morning. Thanks to the modern marvel of social media, however, my thoughts on birthing classes are only a click away because I made the insightful decision to live-tweet all three classes we attended.[1]

What follows are those tweets as well as my thoughts now, after years of experience as a father.

CLASS #1

> **Aaron Sharp** @aaronesharp
> At 1st childbirth class. The first slide is titled contraception…at least there is Wi-Fi.
> 6:57 PM – 7 Mar 2011

At the time, it seemed like perhaps they were showing this slide a little too late. This kind of thing should have been discussed nine months or so earlier. It's a lot like showing someone who is flying in an airplane for the first time that their seat can be used as a flotation device a couple hours after the plane has crash-landed in the ocean. If they don't know at this point, then I'm not sure if there's a point in discussing it.

> **Aaron Sharp** @aaronesharp
> The lady teaching this class is like 14 months pregnant. I hope a live childbirth isn't part of the curriculum.
> 7:07 PM – 7 Mar 2011

Thankfully a live birth was not part of the curriculum. I'm pretty sure I couldn't have handled that. I handled the birth of our children well, but I had to work my way up to it.

ELAINA SHARP CHIMES IN
[1] Good job, hon! I knew your ~~oversharing~~ insight would someday come in handy!

> **Aaron Sharp** @aaronesharp
> A lady in the class has craved Taco Bell. Did I mention that I love my wife?
> 7:15 PM – 7 Mar 2011

A previous chapter discussed cravings and our predilection for Mexican food during pregnancies, but I don't think I could have handled nine months of Taco Bell. Once again, marrying Wonder Woman has proven to be a brilliant move on my part.[2]

> **Aaron Sharp** @aaronesharp
> I think I will add "catheter" to my list of least favorite words.
> 8:07 PM – 7 Mar 2011

This is still true. Sometimes just hearing the word "catheter" makes me a little light-headed. Other entries on my list of least favorite words are "dentist," "methinks," "hernia," "layover," "algebra," and "sputum."[3]

> **Aaron Sharp** @aaronesharp
> I'd like to think I am patriotic, but the lady who wants to deliver a day late so she can deliver on Flag Day is a little crazy.
> 8:13 PM – 7 Mar 2011

God bless America, but the idea of rooting for a baby to stay in your body an extra 24 hours so you could deliver on Flag Day might be an indication that your pregnancy has severely affected your decision-making skills. Christmas I would understand. Saint Patrick's Day if you're Irish, Cinco de Mayo if you are Mexican—these both make sense. Independence Day if you are especially patriotic. But Flag Day?

ELAINA SHARP CHIMES IN

[2] This is why marrying me was a good decision? Really?

[3] Don't forget "moist." I hate the word "moist." Why am I still saying "moist"?

CLASS #2

> **Aaron Sharp** @aaronesharp
> Childbirth class #2, starring a frowning baby made of rubber. Good times.
> 7:00 PM – 14 Mar 2011

The dolls they give you to practice on are not very lifelike. For starters, the inanimate doll is rather docile. It doesn't cry, it doesn't let loose with a bodily function while you are trying to change its diaper, and it isn't offended that you want to put it down. I'm not sure why the rubber faux babies are frowning so much, but I think the manufacturers were trying to simulate a baby's face when it is making a dirty. If so, they succeeded. If they wanted to make this a little truer to life, they would dunk live badgers in grease and let new parents practice on those, but I'm sure that is a liability issue or something.

> **Aaron Sharp** @aaronesharp
> Icebreakers and childbirth classes do not mix.
> 7:14 PM – 14 Mar 2011

I don't like icebreakers to begin with. I don't like them in church, in Sunday school, in Bible study, in community group, at work, at a neighborhood block party, or in any other part of life where people think they are a good idea. For whatever reason, Christians seem overly fond of icebreakers when they get together. I think some people believe that coming up with new and "innovative" ways to break the ice in groups is their spiritual gift. It isn't.

> **Aaron Sharp** @aaronesharp
> Apparently postpartum mood swings are par for the course.[4]
> 7:41 PM – 14 Mar 2011

ELAINA SHARP CHIMES IN

[4] Who you talkin' 'bout, Willis?

I find it funny that this tiny bit of wisdom stuck out to me in the birthing class. My wife is reading this book and contributing some additions, so I will just say that in my experience this was way overblown. Postpartum mood swings are a piece of cake. They are like one of those bananas Foster cakes you can get in a fancy restaurant where the waiter comes out and lights the cake on fire before giving it to you. If the fire doesn't burn the restaurant down, that cake is probably going to be pretty good.[5]

CLASS #3

> **Aaron Sharp** @aaronesharp
> Getting settled in with Mrs. Sharp and our rubber baby again.
> Tonight's topic, lactation…
> 6:57 PM – 21 Mar 2011

Ah yes, lactation. Odds are that a man has never used this word before pregnancy rocked his world. And in my experience, even guys who have been through multiple pregnancies don't utter this word very often. But just know that this rarely spoken word will be very important in the near future. Fight the urge to zone out. Pay attention to this part. The odds of your favorite team winning the championship are much less than the odds that your wife will break down in tears multiple times over lactation. Do yourself a favor and at least pick up enough to know what she is going to be crying about. What you don't pick up in this class, you will have to google later. Trust me, as hard as this is to believe, this is going to be less uncomfortable.

> **Aaron Sharp** @aaronesharp
> To the guy in the front row cuddling with the rubber baby—you, sir, are strange.
> 7:44 PM – 21 Mar 2011

ELAINA SHARP CHIMES IN

[5] How long after one has had a baby can you still call them postpartum mood swings? #askingforafriend

I stand by this comment. This guy was more than a little odd. Pregnancy really seems to bring out strange behavior in some people.

Aaron Sharp @aaronesharp
Well, this has been an awkward video.
8:22 PM – 21 Mar 2011

I'm not going to go into the details of the birthing class video, largely because I have been trying to forget it ever since I saw it. Just know that with years of therapy, counseling from your pastor, and significant intercessory prayer from brothers and sisters in Christ who love you, you might one day recover. It is at least possible.

Aaron Sharp @aaronesharp
This is the twenty-first century. Surely there is a better way to teach this than with hand puppets.
9:01 PM – 21 Mar 2011

I feel like this comment is self-explanatory. If someone sat down and tried to think of the easiest ways to make a birthing class even more awkward than it already was, hand puppets would have to be near the top of the list. Yet there they were.

Aaron Sharp @aaronesharp
The teacher just tried to compare breastfeeding to a basketball hook shot. I have no words.
9:07 PM – 21 Mar 2011

I assumed that the person teaching the class knew something about breastfeeding, or they wouldn't have been in charge of the class. Just know that after four babies, at no point have I ever looked at my wife breastfeeding one of our children and thought, "Man, she really reminds me of Kareem Abdul-Jabbar right now."[6]

> **Aaron Sharp** @aaronesharp
> We just got called out in class because our baby was sitting up on the table signaling touchdown instead of participating in the "cradle."
> 9:21 PM – 21 Mar 2011

This pretty much sums up our time in birthing classes. By the end of class number three, I was so ready to be done that I would have claimed to be pregnant myself if it would have gotten me out of there.

While I was writing this chapter, I asked Wonder Woman for her most vivid recollection of birthing classes. She said she remembered the teacher's instructions about what to do if your water broke so you wouldn't have to come into labor and delivery with a towel wrapped around your waist. And yet the next month, there we were, walking into labor and delivery with a towel wrapped around her waist.[7]

Few things in pregnancy go according to plan. Go to the class, listen, and be prepared for the opposite. Speaking of things not going according to plan, now would be a good time to talk about baby showers.

ELAINA SHARP CHIMES IN

[6] Which is why you are still alive to write this book.

[7] My favorite part of that was the nurse asking me if I was sure that my water broke. Like maybe I just laughed a little too hard and don't know the difference between peeing myself and my water breaking. Then she walked around the desk and saw the puddle I was standing in. Score: Me, 1; nurse, 0.

REGISTERING FOR BABY SHOWERS

If a couple has been married for any amount of time and if the husband is paying even a modest amount of attention, he should have a general idea of the things that make his wife cry. It may not be comprehensive, but a guy usually has a running list in his head (or at least he should) of things that are generally tear-inducing for the love of his life.

Here's how this typically plays out in marriage. Say a loving couple is sitting in the living room watching TV, and the wife goes to the bathroom. While she's in the other room, the husband does a little channel surfing and realizes that *The Notebook* is on channel 27. From that point on in the evening, said husband will avoid channel 27 at all costs. If his wife sees *The Notebook* is on, she is going to want to watch it, and if she watches it, the tears will flow. He avoided what he knew would be the cause of the waterworks, and everything was fine. There were no tears, no boxes of tissues were used, and all was right with the world, or at least for him.

A WIFE'S TEARS

The problem is that when this same husband's wife is pregnant, the list of things that will start the waterworks expands almost infinitely.

To give you as much help as possible, I have created a list of things that might make a pregnant woman cry:

- Everything.

This list is not exaggerated.

Take, for example, the simple—and one would hope, enjoyable—act of registering for baby shower gifts. As a guy, this is one of the more entertaining parts of preparing to be a dad. It doesn't have the weirdness of a visit to the OB/GYN, there are no awkward videos like the ones in birthing classes, and you get to run around the store scanning things with an electronic device. It's like playing laser tag in the store.

> **A pregnant woman will break down in tears for every five items you scan.**

Here is the problem. A pregnant woman will break down in tears for every five items you scan. Sometimes the tears will come from cuteness overload: "Oh, look! Isn't this the cutest little onesie with a monkey on the bottom?" Tears.

Sometimes the tears will be of joy: "I'm just so happy to be having a baby with you!" Tears.

Sometimes the tears will result from exhaustion: "I'm just soooo tired." Tears.

Sometimes the tears will be prompted by hunger: "Why are there no snacks in this store?" Tears.

And sometimes the tears will just be a consequence of being overwhelmed.[1]

Our first experience registering for baby showers included a lot of tears, but the part we both remember was my very pregnant wife being reduced to a sobbing mess by the baby bottle aisle. There were many options. There were bottles that promised to help with colic (false advertising in my experience), bottles that were BPA-free, bottles that regulated temperature, bottles with cute animals on them, bottles that promised to mimic a mother's nipple, and bottles that claimed to ensure that your baby would get into Harvard.

Okay, I made up the Harvard thing, but there were a lot of baby bottles to choose from. It was a baby bottle nirvana, which only served to discourage and overwhelm Wonder Woman.

ELAINA SHARP CHIMES IN

[1] But seriously, *why* are there so many different strollers to choose from? Why can't we just walk in, pick the cutest one, and walk out?

The tears flowed freely. So being the husband that I am, I got her to the rocking chairs as quickly as possible. For my part, I didn't really understand what about baby bottles was so emotional, but by this point in the pregnancy, I at least knew how much I didn't know (everything).

A HUSBAND'S RESPONSE

Here is where the theological reality of the dual roles of husband and father should begin to dawn on future fathers, if it hasn't already. The differences between men and woman have provided material for pastors, comedians, authors, psychologists, and movie directors for decades. Yet in 1 Peter 3:7, the apostle Peter admonishes husbands, "Live with your wives in an understanding way…so that your prayers may not be hindered" (ESV).

People often joke about a husband not understanding his wife's thinking. It's where the old punchline "Can't live with 'em, can't live without 'em" came from. But as it turns out, the joke is on men. God expects husbands to understand their wives. Simply sitting back and saying "I don't get her" doesn't cut it. You can adopt my paternal grandfather's approach and just turn off your hearing aids so you don't have to try to listen to or understand your wife (yes, these are my people),[2] but according to the apostle Peter, doing so means your prayers will be hindered.

What does this theological detour have to do with registering for baby showers? Everything. What are you going to do when you are standing in the middle of a store with a cool little scanner and suddenly your wife—the woman of your dreams and the smartest and most together person you know—is suddenly reduced to a wellspring of tears at the sight of an aisle of baby bottles? You can roll your eyes, or you can actually do your best to try to understand why the baby bottles, the onesie with a ruffle on the bottom, and the 12 shades of blue made her cry.[3]

ELAINA SHARP CHIMES IN

[2] Absolutely one of my favorite Papaw Sharp memories!

[3] Theoretically, of course. If it please the court, I do not recall any time when I cried at onesies with ruffle bums or 12 different shades of blue. And I plead the fifth on crying over baby bottles.

> There's at least a 50 percent chance that even she won't know why she's crying, but your sincere, loving attempt to understand this poor, tissue-codependent woman is a mark of a man ready to take on this challenge.

There's at least a 50 percent chance that even she won't know why she's crying,[4] but your sincere, loving attempt to understand this poor, tissue-codependent woman is a mark of a man ready to take on this challenge. At the baby shower itself, she will cry a couple dozen more times. Getting what you registered for, not getting what you registered for, and getting what you didn't register for will all start the waterworks. And if someone spent dozens of hours making something by hand, there is no chance you will have enough tissues. Just go for a towel.

Through it all, your God-given job is to seek to understand this woman God brought into your life. You are going to be uttering a lot of prayers in the next few months. More than a few will start like this: "Dear God, what have I gotten myself into?" You are going to want the Almighty listening to those prayers, so do yourself a favor and help her with the bottles. Even if you don't get it, making the effort to understand will be good for both of you.

Registering for baby showers is the perfect time to put Peter's words into perspective by taking the leadership in two areas in particular—strollers and lovies.

STROLLERS

There are two good and closely related reasons for you to take the leadership role when it comes to which stroller to register for. First, it is incredibly important, so you need all hands on deck to make sure you get this right. Second, researching which stroller to buy can take a lot of time. If you haven't discovered it by now, pregnancy brain is a real thing.

In our marriage, we had a nice setup for the first five years. Wonder Woman was the brains, and I was the brawn. She handled things like schedules and anything else that had to do with details. I handled big-picture things and moved heavy stuff.

ELAINA SHARP CHIMES IN
[4] True story.

Then she got pregnant, and I found myself having to do some of the thinking for us. It wasn't pretty. A pregnant woman is dog-tired, she has a lot on her mind, and researching things can be stressful for anyone. If you offer to take something off her plate, you will be the hero. Take advantage of the opportunity before she starts mumbling "You did this to me" under her breath over and over again.

> **Then she got pregnant, and I found myself having to do some of the thinking for us. It wasn't pretty.**

So what should you be looking for in a stroller? I'm glad you asked. Focus on these three things:

1. **Wheels**. The bigger the better. You cannot imagine the different surfaces you will be pushing a stroller on. You will need to navigate dirt, gravel, concrete, pavement, rocks, mud, snow, ice, and God only knows what else. Make sure the wheels can handle the load.

2. **Cup holders**. This is easily the most forgotten part of looking at a stroller, and if you don't factor this in, you will regret it. If the stroller is part of your trip, you will need liquid sustenance. Make sure the stroller can handle it. Some strollers don't have many cup holders, but there is some sort of attachment that does. Register for the attachment too.

3. **Turning radius.** Not to get too involved in the physics of vehicles, but turning radius matters a great deal. When you are at the zoo, or Disney World, or the mall around Christmastime with everyone else on the planet, you will greatly appreciate having a highly maneuverable stroller. Take my advice. The first time you take your stroller on an elevator full of people, you will thank me.[5]

ELAINA SHARP CHIMES IN

[5] I would add ease of folding up and putting in the car and storage for *all the bags* when shopping.

LOVIES

A lovey is a blanket, or blanketish cloth, or a stuffed animal known by different names in different families. Some call it a lovey (like our family does), some call it a wubbie, some call it a binkie, and I'm sure there are other names. For the purposes of this chapter, I am just going to go with our family's terminology because I'm the one writing the book.

Kids have various responses to a lovey. They may be attached to it, they may not really care, or their interest may come and go. Because you don't know how much your child is going to care about their lovey, it is best to assume it will be something they obsess over at a level somewhere between unhealthy and obsessive-compulsive. If they aren't into their lovey, there's no harm done, but if they adore their lovey like bees like honey, following these two simple rules will ensure that everything works out just fine.

First, make sure the lovey is machine washable. You can't even imagine everything that will be getting on this thing, so make sure you can just run it through the wash whenever you need to.

> Until you experience it for yourself, there is no way to understand the panic of a parent who suddenly utters the question "Where is the lovey?"

Second, make sure there's a way to attach a GPS locator to the lovey. Until you experience it for yourself, there is no way to understand the panic of a parent who suddenly utters the question "Where is the lovey?" It usually happens after you visit a public place, like an amusement park or the state fair.[6] Everyone involved is hot, cranky, possibly hungry, and definitely tired. You are buckling up the child and turn to the stroller (see, I told you they were important) to get the lovey, but you can't find it.

ELAINA SHARP CHIMES IN

[6] I'm sure every new parent is thinking, "Why would they take their child's cherished lovey to the state fair or the amusement park? It's going to get lost or dirty! We won't be bringing our child's lovey with us to places like that." LOL. Such sweet innocence.

Parents who love each other and promised before God to be together "till death do us part" will start throwing accusations around like they are being interrogated and trying to make sure they aren't the one to go to prison for the crime. "I thought you had it." "*No.* You said you had it." Blood pressures rise, tension mounts…and then hopefully you find the lovey. But this is not guaranteed, which is where the GPS locator comes in handy. Did we spend money on a GPS locator for our lovies? No. So why am I suggesting that you do so? You will understand soon enough.[7]

Now that we've got registering for showers out of the way, that brings us to getting the nursery ready.

ELAINA SHARP CHIMES IN

[7] Here I might add a third suggestion: *Buy multiples of the same lovey.* Because, mark my words, years later when you are scouring the internet to find a replacement lovey that your child will hopefully not notice smells better than different from their lovey, you will have to talk yourself into spending $50 for said lovey replacement. I know you scoff now, but you will understand later.

GETTING THE NURSERY READY

Nurseries have changed over the years. It used to be that a nursery had a crib, probably a rocking chair, and maybe a changing table. The crib probably had some sort of a mobile that was supposed to keep the kid entertained (but rarely did).

But a lot more goes into nurseries in the twenty-first century, especially with the first kid.

ITEMS YOU NEED

> When someone makes the mistake of stepping into the nursery a few hours later, you will swear there are rotting corpses in the room, but the smell is actually much worse.

One indispensable item is the diaper pail. Calling it a pail is a misnomer because while there are several different versions and brands of this device, they all basically function the same way. The diaper pail, in theory, at least gives you somewhere to put used diapers that contains the stench, and then you empty it whenever it starts to get full. Generally, the diaper pail does what it is supposed to, something all too uncommon when it comes to baby products. There are only two real problems with the diaper pail. First, you might forget to hold your breath when it's time to empty the pail. Your nose will never forgive you for this. Second, you might not realize that the lid didn't shut all the way. When this happens and someone makes the mistake of stepping into the nursery a few hours later, you will swear there are rotting corpses in the room, but the smell is actually much worse.

A rocking chair of some sort has been a parenting staple probably since they were invented. I don't have any hard data on this, but movies showing babies in the Old West always included a mom rocking the baby. Movies and television get nothing else right about making and having babies, so I don't know why I am putting any stock in this, but it just seems right. It just seems logical that for hundreds of years, parents have been dealing with fussy babies by using something with a soothing rocking motion. This much even a rookie parent can deduce. This doesn't mean that just any old rocking chair will do. Before purchasing any type of rocker or glider, ask yourself these questions:

- Is this chair comfortable for long periods of time?
- If necessary, could I sleep in this chair for a night or possibly every night for a couple of years?
- Does any part of this chair seem predisposed to squeaking and waking up a child who was just drifting off to sleep? (If the rocking/gliding mechanism of the chair is made of metal, keep WD-40 on hand.)
- Will the color of this chair easily match with a variety of paint schemes? (More on this shortly.)

A crib seems like a must-have, and I am going to give you some credit as a reasonably intelligent person (you purchased this book, after all) and assume that you already knew that. What you may not know about a crib is that to successfully assemble it, you will need a PhD in physics, the patience of Job, as many arms as an octopus, and other people to be beyond earshot so that they cannot hear the words you are mumbling under your breath. Other than that, cribs are a piece of cake.

Baby monitors are a must-have item—except for the fact that they really aren't. Okay, sometimes they are, but not always. Our first house, where the Zoologist and Ballerina had their nurseries, wasn't terribly big. The kids' rooms were right outside the master bedroom, so if a kid sneezed or breathed a little heavily, we heard it with or without a monitor.

Baby monitors are like cars. You can get a basic model that does the job, or you can get a deluxe model that does the job with a lot of bells and whistles. In the world of monitors, the bells and whistles include things such as HD color video, night vision, and text alerts. Parents, especially first-timers, can imagine a thousand nightmare scenarios for which the super-duper-deluxe monitor would be good. If that's you and you've got the money, go for it. But if you don't decide to buy the fancy monitor system, that's okay too. Remember, Jesus's nursery was literally a barn, and He turned out all right. Of course, one of His parents was literally God, but let's not get too deep in the theological weeds.

> Remember, Jesus's nursery was literally a barn, and He turned out all right. Of course, one of His parents was literally God, but let's not get too deep in the theological weeds.

ITEMS YOU DON'T NEED

The thing with the first kid is that you don't really know what you need. Dozens of items you don't really need sound practical or at least plausible, so you register for them (see chapter 9) only to discover that they are as useful as a snowplow in south Texas.

The list of items we jettisoned after our first nursery experience is quite lengthy, but I'll just mention the most disappointing item in the entire nursery: a wet-wipe container that also allegedly warmed the wipes. The wipes weren't warm so much as they were dry. This didn't last very long. When you are wiping bottoms, it is necessary that the wet wipe be both a wipe and wet. If you are missing either of those two elements, things tend to not turn out well. Of all the things that made sense to me before we had a baby, I thought this was a surefire brilliant item. I was wrong.

DECORATING

> When I was a kid, nurseries had themes. The theme was "This is where the baby sleeps."

Another big change in baby nurseries is that now they must have a theme. When I was a kid, nurseries also had themes. The theme was "This is where the baby sleeps."[1] Now things are much more involved. I'm making fun of nursery themes, but it is quite fun to take something you love or want to pass on to your kid and have them enter the world with that thing as a part of their lives. I've always loved vintage aircraft, particularly those from the World War II era, so when we found out our firstborn would be a son, we decided to go with a vintage aircraft theme. My wife was happy, I was happy, everyone was happy.

I'm not sure at what point someone decided that a baby's first room needed a theme, although I am quite certain it wasn't babies making these decisions. For some odd reason, they just don't seem to care. What I do know, however, is who made this call—pregnant women. A woman who is expecting a child quickly realizes that no matter how long "till death do us part" lasts, she will never again have the same leverage as when she is growing another human being inside her body.

> I don't even think "whimsical garden" is a real thing. I think it is something she made up so I wouldn't push back on painting another room.

She knows if she is ever going to get that spare bedroom painted, the best way to do so is to make it the baby's nursery. The nursery's theme is just the cover for her to get her husband to paint the room. When we were pregnant with our first daughter (baby number two, known affectionately as the Ballerina), my wife told me the theme was going to be a "whimsical garden." Surprise, surprise—this involves

ELAINA SHARP CHIMES IN

[1] Careful, dear, your inner old-guy curmudgeon is coming out.

a fresh coat of paint. I don't even think "whimsical garden" is a real thing. I think it is something she made up so I wouldn't push back on painting another room.[2] I'm pretty sure she and all her lady friends got together and had a good laugh over the whole thing. It probably went something like this:

FIRST WOMAN: So how did you get him to paint the room?

WONDER WOMAN: By telling him it was part of the theme, of course.

SECOND WOMAN (laughing maniacally): What did you tell him the theme was?

WONDER WOMAN: Get this. I said it was a whimsical garden. Can you believe it?

THIRD WOMAN: And he bought that? A whimsical garden isn't even a real thing!

ALL THE WOMEN: Men! LOL!

It might not have gone down like that, but I think I'm onto something here. I certainly can't rule it out. Of course, my wife denies this, but that's exactly what she would do if it were true.

But even if my conspiracy theory is accurate, the truth is I have no right to complain. Wonder Woman is a very crafty person, and she handmade a lot of the things we used to decorate our nurseries. She made the bedding for the cribs. She made the curtains for the room. She made a mobile with little faux crystals for one of the girls.[3] She made a wooden propeller for the vintage aircraft room. Okay, the propeller was a Christmas gift from Pops and Nindee, but everything else that involved fabric, sewing, and needles were Wonder Woman originals. She tells me that doing all this by hand saved me a lot of money. I'm not so sure this shows a good grasp of solid fiscal principles, because we still had to buy all the materials,

---

ELAINA SHARP CHIMES IN

[2] But did you die?

[3] Never. Again.

but that isn't the kind of conversation you want to have with a pregnant woman regardless of whether she is the love of your life.

We incorporated a biblical element into every nursery we decorated. Our first-born son shares a name with one of the minor prophets (not Habakkuk), so we put a verse from that prophetic book on the wall of his nursery. He shares a middle name with a famous pastor from years gone by, so we also put a quote by that pastor on the wall. Both of our girls (pregnancies two and three) have Greek names, so we put Bible verses with each of their names in them on their walls. The Jedi shares a name with a prophet as well, so he got a quote from that prophet on his wall. This idea only works with kids with biblical names, but Wonder Woman and I met and fell in love in seminary, so biblical names were just inevitable.[4]

THE TIMING

There's one last thing to talk about when it comes to nurseries. If you are a pregnant woman, just assume this part has nothing to do with you and go on to the next chapter.

Are all the pregnant women gone?

Good, now the rest of us can discuss something.

> You could easily wait until the baby came home from the hospital to start on the nursery, and you'd still be done in plenty of time. Will this argument convince a woman in the throes of pregnancy? Not a chance.

Every pregnant woman is antsy to get the nursery finished. She is convinced that the baby could come at any moment no matter how early along she is in the pregnancy and that because of the imminence of the baby's arrival, the nursery must be finished by about week 20. This is, to be blunt, a case of pregnancy-induced lunacy.[5] Whenever the baby comes, he or she will not be staying in the

---

ELAINA SHARP CHIMES IN

[4] We fully recognize and embrace our seminary nerdiness, so no need to point it out.
[5] Collective gasp from all the pregnant women still reading this chapter!

nursery right away. You could easily wait until the baby came home from the hospital to start on the nursery, and you'd still be done in plenty of time. Will this argument convince a woman in the throes of pregnancy? Not a chance.

Men, you must understand this. The nursery must be treated as the single most important and urgent thing in the history of humanity because your wife is convinced it is. She just knows a baby could pop out of her at any moment and be scarred for life because his or her room was not fully decorated. No woman wants this on her conscience. Besides, a pregnant woman has to have all her friends over so they can see the nursery's theme. Just get it done as fast as possible so your wife is happy and cross it off your to-do list. Because while you are painting that room, she is adding more things to the list.[6]

This brings us to another very important part of this process: revealing the pregnancy to older siblings and explaining to them what is happening.

ELAINA SHARP CHIMES IN

[6] Ahem, did I not "chill out" and "relax" about the nursery with our first child? And then did I not go into labor early? Oh, that's right. I *did* go into labor early. And the nursery was *not finished*. #micdrop

EXPLAINING TO SIBLINGS THAT MOMMY IS GOING TO HAVE A BABY

As an only child who married a middle child, I must confess to being a little bit fascinated by birth order and the impact it has on children. Stereotypes exist for the firstborn, middle children, and the baby of the family. Sometimes these categories are true to form, and sometimes they couldn't be farther from the truth. Whether you are a constantly overlooked middle child, the baby of the family who could do no wrong, or the firstborn who always feels responsible for everything, the moment you found out that Mommy had a baby in her tummy was a life-altering event.

KIDS' REACTIONS

My observations in this chapter are admittedly one-sided. I've never experienced being told that I am being ~~replaced~~ blessed with a sibling, but I have delivered the news to a kid or kids three times now. It must also be noted that in addition to my being an only child, my kids all took the news pretty well, so I am woefully short of horror stories on the topic. Occasionally on social media, someone will post a video of telling their child they are getting a little brother or sister, usually because their child responded in a particularly awful manner. I always have two reactions to these videos.

First, some parents need a better filter for what they put on social media.[1]

Psychologists refer to a firstborn getting additional siblings as "dethronement," which probably is an apt description for a lot of kids. When a kid finds out they are getting a sibling, they find out that their whole world is going to change. Adults are allegedly more mature, but if we got this news on a not-particularly-sanctified day, most of us probably wouldn't handle news like that graciously either. Judging by my social media feed, an awful lot of parents don't react splendidly to a lot of things adults are supposed to be able to handle (unfavorable political news, sports team losses, not getting a parking spot), so maybe we should just give the kids a break.

> Judging by my social media feed, an awful lot of parents don't react splendidly to a lot of things adults are supposed to be able to handle (unfavorable political news, sports team losses, not getting a parking spot), so maybe we should just give the kids a break.

Second, Wonder Woman and I have been very blessed with our kids and their attitudes toward the impending debut of siblings. None of our kids have reacted negatively to the idea of a new baby entering our house. As I write this, the Zoologist is seven years old, and he is still actively trying to convince me that he needs more siblings. For some reason, he thinks we need seven kids. I have explained to him that children are a gift from the Lord, so ultimately this isn't up to me, and it sure isn't up to him, but outside of God just having different plans from mine (not an unusual situation), we are a "four and no more children" family.[2]

The way you tell kids they are going to get a new brother or sister probably doesn't matter. What I mean is, I don't think there is a universal right or wrong way to announce to your kids that the herd is welcoming a new member. But after divulging the impending arrival of another tiny human three times, I have to say that depending on the personality of the kid(s) to whom you are breaking the news, some ways are clearly better than others.

ELAINA SHARP CHIMES IN

[2] Be careful or God might take that as a challenge and add more for our own sanctification. Or for His own amusement.

Some kids are going to be opposed to the idea of anyone or anything else join-ing the family and messing up what they have going on. Especially when a kid is small, there really is only so much you can do to articulate helpfully that this is not the end of the world but is in fact a good thing for them and the entire family. Kids do their own thing, but they also follow their parents' lead a lot more than we realize.

Like a lot of things in life, multiple factors are at play in how you break the news to your children. Here are five things to keep in mind when the time comes to tell kids why Mommy is crying and eating all the chocolate.

Blame God. The last thing you want your kids to think is that they aren't good enough or that they have some deficiency that caused this need to introduce another child to the flock. That is what family yearly performance reviews are for. Seriously though, the earlier you point your kids to the role of God and His sover-eignty in the procreation of the species, the better off you will be. Besides, the last thing you want to do is give a small human who hasn't even made it to kindergar-ten yet a reason to ask you, "Where do babies come from?" The time will come (all too soon in the twenty-first century, by the way) for explaining exactly what role Mommy and Daddy play in conception. For now, quote Psalm 127:3 early and often: "Children are a gift from the LORD; they are a reward from him."

Use analogies, metaphors, and visual aids. Our family has found sonogram pic-tures to be effective tools. A pregnancy is quite an abstract thought for a kid to grasp. It can also be a little difficult for a full-grown man without a baby growing inside of him to wrap his head around, so a child's confusion shouldn't come as a surprise. We were big fans of showing the kids the sonogram picture of their future sibling on an iPad. The first few sonograms don't really look like a baby, so you might have to play this up a little bit, but time is on your side. If they are young and impressionable enough to believe that the tooth fairy is leaving them money under their pillows, you should be able to navigate this topic without an existential crisis.

> A pregnancy is quite an abstract thought for a kid to grasp. It can also be a little difficult for a full-grown man without a baby growing inside of him to wrap his head around, so a child's confusion shouldn't come as a surprise.

Be prepared for your kids' reaction. Don't be surprised if they completely freak out, and don't be surprised if they couldn't care less about what you just said. Maybe they are not old enough to grasp the impact of the situation. A kid may also be excited *until* the new bundle of joy comes home and is constantly screaming and demanding Mommy and Daddy's attention. Then all bets are off.[3]

Be patient. Have fun with it, but remember that even in telling your child or children you are about to add to their number, you are laying the groundwork for future family dynamics. Do your best to make it a joyous occasion, but consider Colossians 3:21: "Fathers, do not exasperate your children, so that they won't become discouraged" (CSB). Enjoy telling your kids and make a memory, but remember everybody has rough days. Odds are you've been told something in the last week that you didn't react to so well either, so try leaning toward compassion and understanding rather than saying, "This meltdown is gonna go viral."

> Giving a small human information and expecting them to keep it quiet is like putting a Great Dane in charge of making sure nobody messes with the steaks.

Wait. Don't tell small children that Mommy is pregnant until you are ready to inform everyone with whom your children come in contact. Giving a small human information and expecting them to keep it quiet is like putting a Great Dane in charge of making sure nobody messes with the steaks. The best you can hope for is that the kids go around telling everyone they have a secret, and it's about Mommy and what's in her tummy. This is the best-case scenario. The worst-case scenario involves them telling their grandparents before you can, the person in line behind you at the grocery store, your pastor, and the stranger walking down the street.

When we found out we were pregnant with our little Jedi, Wonder Woman and I told our parents first.[4] Then, due to unforeseen circumstances that were discussed

ELAINA SHARP CHIMES IN
[3] Don't be surprised if they ask when you can return the baby to the hospital.
[4] *Au contraire, mon frère.* As I just confirmed with my mother, they found out along with all the siblings. I love it when I'm right.

in chapter 11 (pregnancy hormones plus Aaron not handling pregnancy hormones well), we told our kids. We stressed in the strongest possible terms that they were not to tell anyone what we had just told them. They were excited, and we knew the odds were small that they would keep this to themselves, but we had to try. We hadn't even wanted to tell *them* yet, and there were still key people we wanted to tell in person. The next two people our kids saw were Mimi and Opa. The kids greeted them at the door with, "We have a secret that we can't tell you about, but it is about something in Mommy's tummy." I rest my case.

I understand the idea of wanting your children to be the first to know. Just make sure whoever is next on your list gets told shortly thereafter, or you will miss your window of opportunity. This brings us to our next topic: telling immediate and extended family that you are pregnant.

12

TELLING FAMILY

L ots of exciting moments mark a pregnancy. And lots of nerve-racking moments. Sometimes agonizing moments. And there are moments you will remember for the rest of your life. Telling your extended family—parents, siblings, grandparents, and the like—can be all of the above.

> **Here's one of the dirty little secrets of parenting. You love all your kids equally, but you don't always remember the same things about every kid.**

Here's one of the dirty little secrets of parenting. You love all your kids equally, but you don't always remember the same things about every kid. I'm pretty sure this is why kids get complexes, and no doubt when mine read this chapter one day, they will need copious amounts of counseling. As long as they don't expect me to pay for it, I'll be supportive.

We've had four experiences of telling my parents we were expecting. I remember only two of those times (including one when a picture was taken as we said the words). Of the four times we've told my wife's family, I remember only one. This is probably because there is a video of the incident. Does this make me a bad father, a bad son, or a bad son-in-law? Possibly, but I suspect it simply has to do with the fact that as the father of four children, I occasionally forget my children's names and say things like, "Hey, you, stop doing that thing you're doing."

I did my research. I asked my wife when we told people. I called my parents to see if they remembered when we told them we were pregnant with each of the kids. I even asked my in-laws when we told them. In short, I had to spend time researching what happened at four of the happiest moments of my life.

(Spoiler alert: This is what parenthood does to your brain. Anything that happened before parenthood—or after, for that matter—that is not written down somewhere is likely to be forgotten. Half the reason I am writing this book is so I will remember this stuff when I get older. Like 45.)

> **Half the reason I am writing this book is so I will remember this stuff when I get older.**

You may not believe this, but with our first pregnancy, we told my parents at a Mexican restaurant.[1] It wasn't just any restaurant, but my favorite restaurant in my hometown. (Why am I defending my Mexican food consumption? It seems necessary, since it has come up a lot so far and will come up again.)

Anyway, we made a trip to my hometown and broke the news to my parents over nachos. They were excited and cried into their cheese-drenched chips. Not long after, we dropped by my in-laws' house and broke the news to them. Since my wife has siblings and we wanted to do something special for all our future child's aunts and uncles, we made plans for my in-laws to invite everyone out to eat. I'm sure you are dying to know what kind of restaurant it was. All I will say is that the word *hacienda* was in the restaurant's name. We gathered at the restaurant, and the game plan was for my father-in-law to tell everyone to huddle up for a picture, but he was really going to video us telling everyone. Somehow a button didn't get pushed or something like that, and there was no video. Still, despite the absence of videographic evidence, I distinctly remember that it was a happy moment with much laughing and joy. And fajitas.

ELAINA SHARP CHIMES IN

[1] Are you sure? I think we told them at their house. Let's call them and double-check. **Two minutes later** Aaron and his mom think it was at the restaurant. I still disagree.

Telling family about baby number two is fun because you can incorporate your firstborn into the announcement. "Big brother" or "big sister" T-shirts are popular options. If your family doesn't live in your area, you will miss out on the opportunity to tell them in person, but the separation also creates opportunities for creativity. You can allow your oldest child to break the news over a video call; you can take a picture of him or her holding the sonogram photo. My wife informs me that Pinterest is just full of wonderful ideas.

THE THIRD PREGNANCY

By baby number three, people are starting to view your pregnancy announcements with a little less zeal. So it might be time to spice things up a bit. Here's where the calendar can be your best friend. If the timing is right (and it rarely is), you can incorporate holiday festivities into your announcement. We found out we were pregnant for the third time right before Christmas, so we gave my in-laws a family calendar opened to the month of August with the due date circled.[2] For my parents, we got everyone in front of the Christmas tree for a picture. I set the camera timer, rushed to get into the shot, and just as the photo was about to be taken, we said, "We're pregnant!" That was a family Christmas photo we'll never forget.

THREE PLUS

> By baby number four, the extended family is kind of over your propensity to procreate.

By baby number four, the extended family is kind of over your propensity to procreate.[3] At this point, they just assume every time your paths cross, you'll be

---

ELAINA SHARP CHIMES IN

[2] My favorite part about this telling was that it took my dad so long to get it. He looked at the date circled, closed the calendar, and went on to the next gift. **Correction** We just went back and rewatched the video of my dad unwrapping the calendar. *Best. Faces. Ever.* He didn't immediately get that we were announcing another pregnancy, but when he did, it was amazing.

[3] There's a bit of trepidation sharing the big news because there's a chance you might hear something like, "Really? Again? Don't you know why this keeps happening?"

announcing another bun in the oven. You're fertile, they get it. With three kids already running around, you don't really have the time, the energy, or the brain power for big, elaborate announcements. For the fourth time around, I told my parents at one of the Zoologist's soccer games while we were unloading the van. We told Wonder Woman's family during my brother-in-law's birthday dinner.[4] (This time it was Asian, not Mexican.) I think the general response was "Good for you. Please pass the soy sauce."

HURT AND DISAPPOINTMENT

Obviously, this book is generally a lighthearted and—hopefully in its own way—encouraging take on pregnancy, but this is a good place to interject some thoughts on heavier concerns.

Telling family can be tremendously fun and memorable, but it can also be one more tense moment in a nine-month period full of tense moments.

I've already mentioned that we experienced two miscarriages and that pregnancy isn't always a smooth process. Once you've experienced a miscarriage, telling family (and the rest of the world, for that matter) is much more complicated. Do you say something earlier so people can be aware and be praying with you, or do you wait longer so the odds of something going wrong are lessened? I have no idea what to tell you on this one. After our first miscarriage, we told both sets of parents immediately but held off for a while before telling siblings, and we delayed a little longer before we told extended family. Was that a lot of announcing? Yes, but the truth is that having to repeatedly tell people that you miscarried is an awful experience.

> Not everyone will respond to your good news as you would expect or hope.

Even if you are blessed with only relatively easy pregnancies (as if there were such a thing), you need to wrap your brain around this concept: Not everyone will respond to your good news as you would expect or hope.

ELAINA SHARP CHIMES IN
[4] Best birthday gift ever, amiright?

When you tell people you are experiencing the miracle of childbirth again, you anticipate overwhelming joy. But for a variety of reasons, you might get a less enthusiastic reaction. Perhaps Great Aunt Betty will take the announcement as an opportunity to opine about how you shouldn't be having any more kids, since you can't control the ones you already have, or to remind the entire family about the five worst things you did as a kid and how she can't believe that *you* of all people are actually responsible for raising children. This isn't a fun part of pregnancy, and maybe you will be fortunate enough to miss it. But don't be shocked if people feel the need to rain on your parade. Guys, I can all but guarantee this won't bother you to the extent it will bother the saint of a woman carrying your child (see chapter 2 on hormones for further explanation), so you need to be prepared to support your wife. Support in this instance could mean lots of things, but above all, make sure your lovely wife knows you've got her back, preferably with a massage.

> **Support in this instance could mean lots of things, but above all, make sure your lovely wife knows you've got her back, preferably with a massage.**

It's easy to forget that you don't always know what is going on in someone's life, even if you are close to them. For every Great Aunt Betty who, bless her heart, seems intent on functioning as everyone's rain cloud, there is someone else who hears of your pregnancy and experiences mixed emotions. They are happy for you but also struggling to get pregnant themselves. They may not react with overwhelming joy because your happiness is a reminder of their struggle.

As I mentioned in a previous chapter, we tried to get pregnant for six months, had a miscarriage, tried for six more months, and then almost miscarried baby number one. When we started trying for baby number two, we didn't know what to expect, but we got pregnant almost right away. Then my wife miscarried again—on Mother's Day. After some time to recover from that experience, we began to try again, but it didn't happen immediately. We got a call from my wife's brother and sister-in-law one night telling us they were pregnant with baby number three.

I knew this news would make my wife a little sad even though she was happy for her brother and his family, because it was a reminder of the miscarriage and the fact that we hadn't seen the answer to our prayers yet.

The next morning, my wife woke me up by telling me that she wasn't going to let this upset her, that she would be happy for them, and that it would be a lot easier because she just took a pregnancy test and it was positive. I am not always the brightest bulb in the box when I wake up, so it took me a while to grasp what she was telling me. This time God had seen fit to answer our prayers right when it hurt, but that didn't happen every time for us, and I know many people who have tried and tried to get pregnant only to watch everyone around them experience the joy they so desperately wanted to feel themselves.

When it comes time to tell people you are pregnant, have fun, go all out, plan, and scheme to make a great memory. Take videos, take pictures, write it in a calendar, and put kids in *big brother* or *big sister* shirts. Just don't forget that sometimes your piece of good news is a reminder of someone else's piece of bad news.

> **Just don't forget that sometimes your piece of good news is a reminder of someone else's piece of bad news.**

The pregnancy isn't the only news you will have to deliver, which brings us to the gender reveal.

13

FINDING OUT THE BABY'S GENDER

Gender reveals break down into three categories: (1) when the happy couple knows the sex and reveals it to their families, (2) when the wife knows the sex of the baby and the father is the one finding out the gender, and (3) when the couple does not know the sex of the baby, and the doctor holds the baby up and says, "It's a girl!" or "It's a boy!" All three situations will be discussed here.

In recent years, revealing a baby's gender has become quite the production. People have parties with cakes that are either blue or pink under the frosting, or perhaps they put blue or pink balloons in a box and wrap it up as a present to open. As with anything in life, and especially anything involving children, people have started taking things a little too far. Don't believe me? Think I am being a little judgmental about people who happen to like to party a little more than I do?

A CAUTIONARY TALE

I submit to you the case of Dennis Dickey, a US Border Patrol agent. In April 2017, Mr. Dickey and his wife were expecting a baby. They planned a gender reveal party for while he was off duty. This particular gender reveal party would involve Dickey shooting a rifle at a target filled with an explosive substance called Tannerite and colorful packets of powder. Unbeknownst to me, this is a wildly popular thing to do, because the Tannerite company even sells special kits for just such an occasion. I've lived in Texas almost my whole life. I know what Tannerite is. In fact, I have some. Yet somehow, I didn't know there was a market out there for people to find out the gender of their baby with an explosion caused by a gunshot. I also cannot decide if this makes me marvel at what a wonderful time it is to be alive or if it explains a lot about why our world is such a mess.

Anyway, back to Mr. Dickey. He did not know the gender of the child in his wife's womb, and the idea was that he would be the lucky one to fire the gun. The bullet would impact the explosive target, causing a massive blue or pink explosion, and the whole thing would be an amazing story told in the Dickey family for generations to come. Mr. Dickey took careful aim, breathed deeply, and pulled the trigger. His shot was true, and the explosion was accompanied by a beautiful plume of blue.

Don't misunderstand me. I wasn't at this particular gender reveal, but the viral videos of the incident give you a sense of what was going on when, and I quote from the *New York Times* story here, "The target erupted and sparked a fire that consumed more than 45,000 acres of land and resulted in more than $8 million in damages,"[1,2] In October 2018, Dickey pled guilty to a misdemeanor violation of Forest Service regulations for starting a fire that 800 firefighters battled for a week.

> If there is a way that your gender reveal can go wrong and result in your spending $100,000 as the first of many payments for restitution, then—and I'm just throwing this out there as a possibility—maybe you should rethink your plans.

This seems like common sense, but let me just make sure we are all on the same page here. If there is a way that your gender reveal can go wrong and result in your spending $100,000 as the first of many payments for restitution, then—and I'm just throwing this out there as a possibility—maybe you should rethink your plans. I'll be the first to admit that I don't completely understand the lengths

---

ELAINA SHARP CHIMES IN

[1] That is one expensive baby on the way!

[2] Melissa Gomez, "Border Patrol Agent's Gender-Reveal Party Sparked Arizona Fire, Lawyer Says," *New York Times*, October 1, 2018, https://www.nytimes.com/2018/10/01/us/gender-reveal-arizona-fire.html.

to which people go just to say "It's a boy" or "It's a girl," but unless you can afford the $8 million fine, maybe it's best to pare down those elaborate plans and stick with the cake idea.

KEEP IT SIMPLE

When we found out that our firstborn was going to be a boy, we bought these little "It's a Boy!" signs on toothpicks.[3] Shortly thereafter, my parents visited, so we took them to a restaurant named Blue Goose, which as you might have guessed serves Mexican food. We ordered the appetizers, and I made an excuse to leave the table to ask the waiter to put some of the "It's a Boy!" signs in the nachos, tamales, or whatever appetizer we ordered.

When we told my in-laws, we met them at an Italian restaurant that has paper you can write on covering the tables. We got there before my in-laws and wrote "It's a Boy!" on the paper under the plates. At some point in the evening whenever they moved their plates, they saw that we were having a boy, and much joy and bruschetta ensued.

> God has given you the responsibility of raising another human from birth, and thanks to the wonder of modern technology, you can already begin praying specific prayers for the child four to five months before they ever leave the womb.

Finding out the gender of a baby is a marvelous thing. God has given you the responsibility of raising another human from birth, and thanks to the wonder of modern technology, you can already begin praying specific prayers for the child four to five months before they ever leave the womb. As an expectant father of a son, I prayed that my son would not be like me, and as the expectant father of a daughter, I prayed that my daughter would watch out for boys like me.

ELAINA SHARP CHIMES IN

[3] We were recent seminary graduates, just struggling to make ends meet, so even buying these was a budget stretcher.

PLANNERS AND NONPLANNERS

As you've probably guessed by now, Wonder Woman and I both wanted to know the genders of our babies as soon as possible.[4] This is a personal preference, but if you go the route we did, let me offer one word of caution. We found out that we were going to be having a baby boy via the sonogram. My lovely wife was pumped. No, that doesn't quite do her mood justice. She was bouncing off the walls with excitement. Her happiness was adorable—until the doctor came in and took her blood pressure. As it turns out jumping up and down and yelling "We're having a boy! We're having a boy! We're having a boy!" raises one's blood pressure more than a little bit.[5] And if there's one thing that OB/GYNs don't like seeing, it is high blood pressure from a pregnant lady. The moral to the story here is that if you are a pregnant woman who is going to find out the gender of your baby, it would probably be advisable to get the doctor to take your blood pressure before the revelatory moment.

> If you are one of those couples who goes the entire pregnancy without knowing the gender of your baby, I feel it is only fair to tell you that I just don't understand you at all.

If you are one of those couples who goes the entire pregnancy without knowing the gender of your baby, I feel it is only fair to tell you that I just don't understand you at all. Let me be clear. I'm not being judgmental. There is enough of that in pregnancy and parenting as it is. I just have a hard time wrapping my brain around your decision-making paradigm. I've had friends who have done this, and even after they articulate their reasoning, I'm left scratching my head and wondering what it is like in their world. I'm a planner by nature. When I was a child growing up, my dad would often tell me, "Plan your work, and work your plan." And in my marriage, I am nowhere near the bigger planner of the two of us.

ELAINA SHARP CHIMES IN

[4] I respect and admire greatly the women who can wait nine months to discover the gender of their baby. Alas, I am not one of them. As was previously shared, the nursery needs to be planned!

[5] Stupid blood pressure.

But if this anything-goes, fly-by-the-seat-of-your-pants philosophy is how you approach life and, as a result, pregnancy, I wish you the best. Just know that I may not be the guy to come to for advice. I have no doubt that people who are somehow able to magically go about their pregnant lives without knowing the gender of their future child are content with their choice. They all seem happy and well adjusted while patiently waiting until the child emerges from the birth canal and the doctor announces pink or blue. If this is what works for you, by all means go for it.

WORDS OF WARNING

For the rest of us who like to know as much as we can about what is coming and plan accordingly, I would like to offer three pieces of food for thought.

First, the sonogram method of gender prediction is very accurate. Depending on where you read the statistics, most of which I suspect are being made up on the spot, sonograms are right as much as 97 percent of the time or possibly as low as 90 percent of the time. Either way, that is a wonderfully high percentage—unless you are one of the 3 to 10 percent. What I am trying to tell you is to have confidence in what the sonogram says, but keep your receipts just in case.

Second (soapbox warning), can we all please stop with the "girls are expensive" jokes when we find out someone is having a baby girl? I'm the father of two sons and two daughters, and you know what they all have in common? They are all expensive. Becoming a parent means signing up to be bled dry—financially, emotionally, physically, mentally…you name it. God has called you to pour yourself out for your kids, so let's stop acting like one gender somehow puts a special burden on the family. Studies have shown that from birth to age 18, the average child costs parents well over $200,000. *They. Are. All. Expensive.* And they are all worth it. If you wanted to add an inexpensive member of the family, you should have bought a goldfish. (Soapbox finished.)

> If you wanted to add an inexpensive member of the family, you should have bought a goldfish.

Third, childbirth is a miracle, and few things exhibit the sovereignty of God more than the gender of a child. You do nothing to pick or influence this; it is all in God's hands. That means if you are a dad who desperately wants a little boy to play catch with, but you find yourself as the dad of five girls, God knew what He was doing. Or if you are a mom who has been dreaming of dressing a little girl in dresses and pigtails for years, yet you are the mom of smelly, stinky, sweaty boys, your predicament is all part of God's sovereign plan. Knowing this doesn't make it any easier to deal with frustrated expectations, but it is helpful in parenting to secure yourself to the idea that God does not make mistakes.

Just make sure you take it easy on the exploding gender reveals. Which brings us to a deeper discussion of sonograms.

SONOGRAMS

Before going through pregnancy, it is possible to believe that here in the twenty-first century, our scientific understanding of the human body and its processes is so fully developed that the medical profession is a well-oiled machine. Nothing will disabuse you of this notion faster than going to your first sonogram.

To be clear, I am not disparaging OB/GYNs and the medical professionals who perform sonograms. We had the same nurse perform almost every sonogram we had for four pregnancies. She was a wonderfully sweet lady whom we knew well by the time our Jedi was born. She was able to see all sorts of things in a sonogram that I took her word for because I had no idea what I was looking at. I'm still not entirely sure that the first few sonograms aren't just showing us grainy black-and-white footage of a bean, but if the insurance company is convinced enough by the procedure to pay for it, there must be something to it.

> I'm still not entirely sure that the first few sonograms aren't just showing us grainy black-and-white footage of a bean, but if the insurance company is convinced enough by the procedure to pay for it, there must be something to it.

Over the last few years, 3D and even 4D ultrasounds have become somewhat popular during pregnancies. I am not a medical professional, but some medical professionals suggest these aren't advisable. I'll just leave you to do your own research before you get one. We didn't get this type of ultrasound primarily because of a simple question: Is this covered by insurance? The answer for us was no, which meant we were just fine with the grainy black-and-white images.

WHY MEN DON'T GET PREGNANT

To have an ultrasound, everyone involved gathers in a room that, as I've mentioned in a previous chapter, is very strange and foreign to a first-time dad. You and your wife are both very excited to see this first image of the amazing act of creation God has performed. I'll not get into the specifics of exactly how this procedure is conducted, but let's just say that one of the most amazing things about women in general, and particularly a pregnant woman, is just how much they are able to endure. The amount of poking, prodding, probing, and pinching a woman undergoes, let alone the pain and discomfort of carrying and delivering a child, would discourage a man from ever becoming pregnant if the roles were reversed.[1] If you doubt it, let me let you in on a little secret: Lots of men skip their yearly physicals, and a big reason is that they don't want to get their prostate checked. According to the American Cancer Society, one in nine men will be diagnosed with prostate cancer in their lifetime, and yet an inordinate number of men decide they'd rather not endure the uncomfortable test. If men were the ones who got pregnant, humanity would have died out before we got halfway through the book of Genesis. The Bible would be very short, and there would be a verse that said, "And thus the human race ended with Jacob."

> If men were the ones who got pregnant, humanity would have died out before we got halfway through the book of Genesis.

Speaking of the patriarchs, sonograms are one of those things that will leave you with an immense amount of thankfulness and respect for women, who have been

---

ELAINA SHARP CHIMES IN
[1] Word.

giving birth for thousands of years without high-tech medical advances. Think of Isaac and Rebekah. Rebekah struggles with twins in her womb, and this is how The Message translation puts it:

> Isaac prayed hard to GOD for his wife because she was barren. God answered his prayer and Rebekah became pregnant. But the children tumbled and kicked inside her so much that she said, "If this is the way it's going to be, why go on living?" (Genesis 25:21-23 MSG).[2]

Rebekah is in agony as two human beings inside her struggle for control. The imagery of two boys in a womb tumbling and kicking is eye opening. I have no idea how thousands of years ago she had any idea what was happening, but she did. Pregnancy in the modern era is full of anxious moments. What must it have been like when you didn't have the testing and the wonderful grainy pictures to track your child's growth? There are so many twists and turns to pregnancy that it's almost incomprehensible how people managed to navigate these nine months before we had the technology we have now. Sudden pains and sensations begin for no apparent reason. Previous pains and sensations that had become like old friends are now inexplicably not there. A million reasons present themselves to call the OB/GYN in a panic. Yet until the last 50 years or so, all of it was done with very little technological expertise.

Now you go into a room and they tell you how much the baby weighs, how big the head is, how much fluid surrounds the baby, how long its tiny little femur is, and a host of other pieces of information you didn't know you needed to know. Sonograms can show reasons for concern, but it's comforting to know the problem or concern can be tracked and monitored. Be glad you are experiencing this phase of life now and that you aren't living in a tent next door to Isaac and Rebekah a few thousand years ago. I'm guessing those nine months weren't pleasant for anybody within earshot.

ELAINA SHARP CHIMES IN

[2] I never had twins, but I completely feel Rebekah's pain here. All four of my babies were world-champion kickers.

A DOSE OF REALITY

> The first sonogram is a little anticlimactic because, the truth is, they could be showing you stock footage of almost anything, for all you know.

The first sonogram is a little anticlimactic because, the truth is, they could be showing you stock footage of almost anything, for all you know. They point at a little bubble on the screen and tell you a bunch of statistics about your baby, but you are staring at the screen thinking, "Okay, if you say so, but I'm not totally sure you aren't just showing me a stray pea from lunch." As the months go by, the grainy black-and-white pictures of beans look more and more like something else—an alien. This isn't a popular viewpoint, because there's a wonderful sentimental aura about pregnancy, but listen to me on this one.

Everyone is convinced that their baby is beautiful and that even in the womb he or she is the most adorable thing God ever created.[3] I am convinced that this is part of a God-given parental instinct that tells you your baby is much more special than anyone else on the planet believes it to be. When the child is born, this same instinct tells you your baby is the cutest ever, which is not true because all four of ours were cuter. It tells you that despite all the crying and screaming, your child is the best-behaved baby. Once again, the odds are against your being right. It tells you that your child is probably going to be an intellectual prodigy because he or she smiled at you at only three weeks old. But that was just because the child was pooping.

When you see those first few sonogram pictures, you may say things that sound silly or that indicate you need to seek professional counseling. You will say, "He has your nose," or "She has your chin." But the truth is, the prospect of parenthood has turned you into an insane person who is capable of great depths of self-deception. At 20 weeks, the baby doesn't resemble one side of the family, because

---

ELAINA SHARP CHIMES IN

[3] Ours really were the most adorable! Take the Zoologist, for example. We have a sonogram of his profile where he is *praying*! I'm talking hands clasped together under his chin, full-on praying.

at this point the baby more closely resembles E.T. than any blood relative. Unless of course your Uncle Fred looks like E.T., in which case it is entirely possible that your baby favors Uncle Fred.[4]

> At 20 weeks, the baby doesn't resemble one side of the family, because at this point the baby more closely resembles E.T. than any blood relative. Unless of course your Uncle Fred looks like E.T., in which case it is entirely possible that your baby favors Uncle Fred.

There is now a blood test that can determine the sex of an in utero child at 10 or 12 weeks, but as you might have guessed, it isn't always covered by insurance. However, as I mentioned in chapter 13, most people find out about the gender through sonograms, which are usually accurate. Keep this in mind when you go to find out the sex of your child, because the person conducting the sonogram is going to point to the presence or absence of a particular male body part as proof positive. If they proclaim the baby a boy, you will look at the allegedly foolproof evidence and wonder, "But are we sure that is what we're looking at? Could it possibly be a hand or something? After all, the little guy is squished in there." The OB/GYN will assure you this is a done deal, possibly even while patting you on the head. Just remember, before you start buying blue paint, there is a 3 to 10 percent chance that it was a hand, finger, or some other body part. Just hedge your bets—that's all I'm saying.

Now that we have discussed gender and sonograms, this brings us to a very important part of pregnancy—nesting.

ELAINA SHARP CHIMES IN

[4] And don't be scared if this alien resemblance doesn't go away at birth either. One of our children came out with a cone head akin to Dan Aykroyd.

NESTING

One of the foundations of proper communication is making sure everyone understands the definition of the terms being used. So before we get into this chapter, let's take a stab at defining what exactly it is we are talking about when we mention nesting.

> I estimate that 27.8 percent of pregnant women try to throw away their husbands while nesting. Most of the time they are unsuccessful.

A pregnant woman, who by all accounts should be off her feet letting other people clean, is nesting when she spends excessive amounts of time and energy cleaning, organizing, recleaning, reorganizing, and purging everything in sight. This nesting is primarily focused on her own domicile, but it will eventually spill over to family-owned vehicles, her workplace, and anywhere she may believe her new child will spend any amount of time. I estimate that 27.8 percent of pregnant women try to throw away their husbands while nesting. Most of the time they are unsuccessful.

THE TIDINESS GAP

Whenever you start making generalizations about men, women, and marriages, you are bound for trouble, because no two people are alike and no two marriages are alike. Still, I think I am on safe ground when I say that generally when two people get married, one of them usually likes things tidier and more organized than the other. This is what I am going to call the "tidiness gap."[1] The tidiness gap is small in some marriages, and in others it is a gulf the size of the Grand Canyon.[2] It also seems to me, based on my own observations, that the male is usually the one behind in the tidiness gap. No doubt my own experiences color my thoughts on this topic, but I think I'm on to something.

Here's how this typically plays out in the Sharp household. Wonder Woman and I currently live in a house with four small humans seven years old and under. I say "currently" because time will elapse between when I write these words and when this book is published, so they will be older by the time you are reading this. Also, I say "currently" because with the way this week has gone, the odds of one or more of our children going to military school are reasonably high, and I want to give myself some wiggle room.

Four children in a home smaller than the Biltmore Estate means that noise, messes, and general chaos are our constant companions. For me, this is an inconvenient part of our lives right now. Occasionally it will grate on my nerves, but that is the exception to the rule. Wonder Woman, however, has a much different, more visceral reaction to the repeated verbal and visual assaults we are subjected to daily.

I will see a messy room and think, "This room is messy. It would be great to get it picked up. I also need to finish writing a chapter, get the trash out by the curb, change the lightbulb in the utility room, pay the bills, and try to get some time on the exercise bike." My brain then prioritizes this list. The items with deadlines move to the front of the line, and after that it mostly comes down to pain points and return on the investment of time and energy. By the time I've run my internal calculus, the messy room doesn't seem so bad, and I make my peace with it for a little while longer. My brain files it in the "Well, you've got four kids" file, and I move on. I'll get around to tidying it after I've dealt with other, more pressing things.

ELAINA SHARP CHIMES IN

[1] More like the "Tidiness Grand Canyon" at our house. But I still love you anyway.

[2] Well, at least we agree. Also, I would like to point out that I made the previous footnote before reading this sentence. We work well together.

In some ways, marriage is two people loving each other because of (and despite) a cornucopia of differences.

But one of the biggest things you learn about God when you promise another flawed human being "till death do us part" is just how different two people can be. There are gender differences, personality differences, birth-order differences, and all sorts of others. In some ways, marriage is two people loving each other because of (and despite) a cornucopia of differences. Which is a rather long-winded way of saying when Wonder Woman sees a messy room, her beautiful, God-given brain does an entirely different set of calculations than mine. While my brain is running numbers and figuring the return on the investment, her brain says, "This room is messy. *This* room is messy. *This room* is messy. *This room is* messy. *This room is messy!* THIS. ROOM. IS. MESSY!" Other needs—the trash that needs to be taken out, the lightbulb that needs to be changed, and the bills that need to be paid—magically disappear as if riding a fiery chariot to heaven with the prophet Elijah. All she can see, all she can think about, all she can focus on is the messy room. It is just how she is wired.

And this is before nesting.

SURVIVING NESTING

When nesting, a pregnant woman's desire to clean and organize is magnified no less than ten times. It may be a hundred times.

When nesting, a pregnant woman's desire to clean and organize is magnified no less than ten times. It may be a hundred times. It's like standing on the ground and seeing a rocket blast into outer space. There is a certain point at which the rocket is so far above you, you can't really conceptualize the distance. This is what happens with nesting and the tidiness gap.

If a man married to a pregnant woman had written the King James Version,

Ecclesiastes 12:12 would say, "And further, by these, my son, be admonished: of the cleaning there is no end; and much organizing is a weariness of the flesh."

On one hand, it is an amazing sight to behold, because this human being who is growing another human being inside of her and is already exhausted somehow finds untapped reserves of energy to mop the kitchen for the fifth time this week—and it's only Tuesday. On the other hand, her back hurts, her ankles are swollen, and she is uncomfortable 100 percent of the time, yet you find her on her hands and knees cleaning under the couch. For a lot of women, nesting borders on compulsive behavior. But listen to me carefully—don't dare suggest anything like that out loud, or you will wake up one morning to find yourself on the curb with the trash waiting to be picked up by the garbage truck.[3]

Just like it isn't always the woman who is the neat freak of the house, not every pregnant woman nests. But it happens enough that as the husband and father-to-be, you should at least be aware of the warning signs so you can respond accordingly.

NESTING INDICATORS

Here are five indicators that a pregnant woman is nesting or is about to begin nesting.

First, you see her opening a container of cleaning fluid, such as detergent or dish soap, just to smell it. The more something like this happens, the surer you can be that nesting is indeed taking place. Also, you would do well to make a trip to the grocery store to stock up on whatever organic cleaning supply she loves to smell. Consider using it as cologne.

Second, she mentions repeatedly that the paint needs touching up around the house. (For what it's worth, if you don't do this, she probably will. And I know what you are thinking—that would save you the trouble of having to do it. Trust me on this one—if your pregnant wife does touch-up painting around the house because you are too lazy or not interested enough to get it done, this is not a point in your favor.)[4]

ELAINA SHARP CHIMES IN

[3] Amen and amen.

[4] I don't remember touching up paint while I was pregnant. Are you giving this as a real example or a theoretical example?

> Trust me on this one—if your pregnant wife does touch-up painting around the house because you are too lazy or not interested enough to get it done, this is not a point in your favor.

Third, she is constantly muttering to herself about how the vacuum, dishwasher, washer, or any other cleaning implement is not working as well as it used to. If you make it through multiple pregnancies without purchasing another vacuum cleaner, you should consider yourself a man of rare talents and abilities. I was not a man of rare talents and abilities.

Fourth, you notice that you are suddenly getting a lot of mail from the Container Store. Pay attention, and after a while, you will notice these catalogs have pages with corners turned down and things circled. Eventually you will see little sticky notes sticking out of the pages. If you think you can get away with it, throw these catalogs out with the trash. Just know that after you do this a few times, she will be on to you. You will have simply delayed the inevitable.

Fifth, you hear your wife say more than once, "You know, cleanliness is next to godliness."[5] Here is where you must pay close attention. If you are a good husband who strives to honor and glorify God, who wants to be the spiritual leader in his family, who takes his relationship with God seriously and hopes that his family does as well, you are going to be tempted to say something along the lines of "Well, you know honey, that isn't actually in the Bible." I am sure you would say it in all honesty and sincerity, but do not do it. It's a trap. Don't fall for it. If a pregnant woman believes that the Scriptures teach that the whole house must be dusted three times a week, save your impeccable theology for another time and get to work dusting. Do not correct her theology unless it reaches the point of full-blown heresy, and even then, consider having your pastor (or even better, an older woman in the church) talk to her about it. Unless your favorite commentary makes a good pillow while sleeping on the couch, just wait and have this deep, Spirit-filled conversation some other time.

ELAINA SHARP CHIMES IN

[5] Okay, I know I never said that. Or did I?

> If a pregnant woman believes that the Scriptures teach that the whole house must be dusted three times a week, save your impeccable theology for another time and get to work dusting.

A nesting woman's hormones are going crazy, and she is being compelled by an almost obsessive desire to clean. She might overdo it, or other things might be going on, which brings us to bed rest.

BED REST

Bed rest is not something that will be part of every pregnancy. Like other elements of pregnancy, we are going to attempt to find the humor in it, but that doesn't change the fact that it is full of seriousness and will spur a consistent prayer life.

Pregnancies very rarely play out the same way. With our first pregnancy, bed rest was never even mentioned. Then came pregnancy number two and the Ballerina.

THE NUMBERS

One of the things that happens with pregnancy is that at least in the beginning, you can become a little obsessed with the numbers. Human chorionic gonadotropin—HCG—is a hormone produced during pregnancy in the cells of the placenta. Progesterone numbers indicate levels of progesterone—a hormone released by the corpus luteum in the ovary. Both numbers, as well as a few others, are very important to the health of mom and baby, so you spend a lot of time watching, thinking about, and praying about the numbers.

Throughout our second pregnancy, some of Wonder Woman's numbers had been inching the wrong direction,[1] so we weren't totally surprised when the doctor said she would need to go on bed rest. We headed home from the OB/GYN's office trying to figure out how we could keep my wife in bed and resting with as little stress

---

ELAINA SHARP CHIMES IN

[1] Namely, my blood pressure.

as possible.[2] We set up a rotating cast of friends and family who could stay with her and our always busy one-year-old Zoologist during the day while I was at work.

A week later, we went back to the doctor, hoping we could continue doing bed rest at home. I was in the lobby trying to keep the Zoologist entertained when Wonder Woman called me on my cell phone. When I answered the phone and heard tears, I knew it wasn't good. As it turns out, her week of bed rest at home hadn't included enough rest or enough bed. Now at 35 weeks, she was being admitted to the hospital for the rest of her pregnancy.[3]

It was about this time I realized I was in over my head in life. You can "fake it until you make it" for a while as a new husband, but pregnancy largely ends that fantasy, especially when bed rest is involved. Now I had a wife in the hospital, a kid to take care of, and a job to work. All this while running numbers in my head about deductibles, calendar year out-of-pocket maximums, and short-term disability benefits. This is the moment when a man is officially, inescapably an adult. Play all the video games you want, but at this point you might as well be your dad, because you are adulting, and there is nowhere to hide.

> This is the moment when a man is officially, inescapably an adult. Play all the video games you want, but at this point you might as well be your dad, because you are adulting, and there is nowhere to hide.

This is also the moment you realize just how much you rely on God and how much you need help. Sometimes early adulthood can lull you into thinking you have things figured out. Then comes this situation where the doctor uses phrases like "medically necessary" and "for the health of mom and baby." Suddenly you realize that you don't have things figured out and that the entrance of a new life into the world really is a miracle. If anything in pregnancy will drive you to your knees, it is bed rest.

ELAINA SHARP CHIMES IN

[2] This was going to be interesting given our very active almost-two-year-old.

[3] Actually, I followed all the doctor's instructions, thank you very much. It just didn't help.

THE CALLS FOR HELP

Even though it was an "I'm definitely an adult now" moment, that doesn't mean I was beyond asking for help. My first call was to my in-laws. They needed to know their daughter was going into the hospital, and I figured the one of us who wasn't crying should make the call. I also asked if they could keep the Zoologist for the night so I could spend the first night at the hospital with Wonder Woman. My second call was to my parents. This call was the verbal equivalent of a Bat-Signal for Mimi. I'm thankful my dad can survive on sandwiches and scrambled eggs, because I needed my mother more at that moment than he did. At the time, my parents lived six hours from us. We made plans for Mom to head our way the next morning. I could (mostly) handle the nights and weekends, but we would need someone to keep the Zoologist, possibly for a few weeks, while I was at work during the day. Little-known fact: One-year-olds aren't really that helpful at information technology.

(Side note: As I'm writing this, it boggles my mind that at the time I considered this a high degree of difficulty. We had one child. One. Now with four kids running around, whenever we have time with just one child, it is a breeze. But back then, having to handle a one-year-old by myself seemed like such a big deal. I thought I must be some sort of superdad who was winging it with one kid by himself without a wife to make sure he kept the baby alive. Now if I end up wrangling only two kids, I look at it as a mini vacation.)

> That night left an indelible impression on me, not for sentimental reasons, but because the hospital apparently purchased its furniture in a closeout sale from the Spanish Inquisition.

I got the Zoologist to my father-in-law, packed a bag for myself, and headed back to spend the night in a hospital room with my very pregnant, extremely emotional, and stressed out (even though she wasn't supposed to be) wife. I will never forget that night as long as I live. You might assume that was because it was an emotional and wonderful time as we neared the birth of our daughter. If so, you couldn't be wronger. That night left an indelible impression on me, not for sentimental reasons, but because the hospital apparently purchased its furniture in a closeout sale from the Spanish Inquisition. The "couch" that stretched out into a "bed" was a lot of things, but comfortable furniture was not one of them. In the middle of the night, I pondered driving back home to get my wife's pregnancy pillow but thought better of it because five pregnancy pillows wouldn't have made that thing comfortable. Also, Wonder Woman would have strangled me.[4]

THE CONTEST EVERY MAN LOSES

I woke up the next morning after a fitful night of sleep with my left shoulder hurting. I didn't think much of it at the time, but over the next few days, rather than subsiding, the pain began to increase. Eventually I saw a doctor who informed me that I had a tear in my shoulder. That's right, I injured my shoulder sleeping at the hospital with my wife, who had just gone on bed rest. Honestly, this probably says more about me than it does the bed rest, but I'm telling you, a couple more nights on that "bed" and two of us might have been on bed rest.

> There is no amount of physical pain a man can endure while his wife is pregnant that is acceptable for him to complain about.

It also bears mentioning here that there is no amount of physical pain a man can endure while his wife is pregnant that is acceptable for him to complain about.[5] No matter what it is, if a man verbalizes something about physical pain or discomfort while his wife is with child, his wife will immediately set him straight on who has it tougher right then. As a husband, if you have a headache, hers is worse, and it has been ongoing for four months. If your back hurts, you don't know the meaning of back pain. If a man gets run over by a bus while saving a small puppy and

---

ELAINA SHARP CHIMES IN

[4] I'm sorry that your one night on an uncomfortable sofa couch scarred you for life. It must have been much worse than trying to sleep with a hurricane in your belly for nine months.

[5] Exactly.

narrowly lives to tell the tale, it would be better for him to say "I feel fine" than to express any sort of sentiment that can be construed by his wife as complaining about his physical state.[6]

The idea behind bed rest is that because the pregnant woman has been taken off her feet and restricted from working or doing anything that requires exertion, she will be better physically and, as a result, so will the baby in her womb, who relies on the woman's health and safety to grow to full term. The problem with this is that bed rest is very stressful for a pregnant woman.[7]

> Even knowing the necessity of bed rest, women tend to find the inactivity and restrictions almost unbearable. In the exact same situation, a man would be as relaxed as he has ever been in his life. Eventually the doctor would have to induce labor if for no other reason than to get the man to get out of bed and out of the hospital.

Here is another place where men and women differ. The only way a pregnant woman can be convinced to go on bed rest is by a cadre of medical professionals explaining that the bed rest is necessary for her health and the health of the baby. Even knowing the necessity of bed rest, women tend to find the inactivity and restrictions almost unbearable. In the exact same situation, a man would be as relaxed as he has ever been in his life. Eventually the doctor would have to induce labor if for no other reason than to get the man to get out of bed and out of the hospital. Then again, all they would have to do is make him spend the night on one of those pull-out beds, and any sane human being would gather their doesn't-quite-cover-everything gown around them and flee the hospital as quickly as possible.

By the time we endured our second bed rest, we were a little more prepared for

---

ELAINA SHARP CHIMES IN

[6] Hmph. You make me sound like I have no sympathy at all.

[7] Don't tell my husband, but bed rest didn't end up being that bad. Especially when it was for our third baby and I had two toddlers at home. I practically got to have a vacation during the most exhausting and uncomfortable time of the pregnancy.

the experience, but only a little. With our second bed rest, we already had a four-year-old and a two-year-old at home. The whole family was eagerly anticipating the arrival of the third member of the Sharp brood, and then suddenly Mommy was staying at the hospital instead of coming home. Two things bear mentioning here.

First, it might surprise or possibly offend some people that I used the phrase "our bed rest." Believe me, I have a great appreciation for what women go through when they are pregnant. I think I've been pretty clear in stating there is literally nothing a man could ever do that would compare with the pain, suffering, and agony of growing another human being in your body and delivering that baby. That being said, when a woman with kids gets pregnant, the husband becomes much more involved in the pregnancy, and this involvement grows with every child. During our first pregnancy, I wrote my first book. Wonder Woman was so tired, she was asleep most nights by nine, so I would stay up late writing. Think of that. I had so much time on my hands, I literally wrote a book. But when Mommy is in the hospital for two weeks and Daddy is the one responsible for taking care of Mom and the two kids, I think it is fair to say he has a sliver of ownership in this project. That isn't to suggest the shares are equal, but when there is a baby to grow and two small kids to take care of, this is definitely a team effort.

Second, while my wife was in the hospital, she always had her laptop and some files with her to work on as needed during the day. The kids caught on that Mommy was working while she was in the hospital, and for the longest time they called it "Mommy's office." Every night they'd ask me when we were going to see Mommy in her office again.

The two weeks Wonder Woman spent in the hospital on bed rest with baby number three, the Fashionista, were among the most stressful two weeks for me of all four pregnancies. But we survived, and the twitching has almost gone away completely. Just thinking about it while writing this chapter has me on edge. It's probably time to move on to a lighter subject—unsolicited advice.

UNSOLICITED ADVICE

After a couple announces they are expecting a baby, they will experience approximately six minutes of peace before the unsolicited advice begins. Actually, it's probably less than that. At first the advice is just a trickle, as only those in your immediate sphere pontificate about what is best for you and baby. But as a woman begins to show and the pregnancy becomes more apparent, you will notice that friends, immediate family, coworkers, distant relatives, the waiter at your favorite restaurant, the checker at the grocery store, that friend from high school you haven't seen in a decade but are Facebook friends with, and random people at the mall see the pregnancy belly and believe unsolicited advice floodgates are open.

On one hand, most of these people are well meaning and sincere, and the book of Proverbs does say, "Without consultation, plans are frustrated, but with many counselors they succeed" (Proverbs 15:22 NASB). Shouldn't you be excited to be the recipient of all this wonderful advice given to you free of charge? Maybe, but let's not forget that the book of Proverbs also says, "The more talk, the less truth; the wise measure their words" (Proverbs 10:19 MSG).

As a man, you need to understand a few things about dealing with unsolicited advice. You have an important role to play to ensure your wife's mental well-being.

TAKING ONE FOR THE TEAM

First (not to be repetitive, but this is important enough to reiterate), pregnancy impacts your wife physically, mentally, and emotionally. She is stressed, she feels awful, her hormones are raging, she can't sleep…and that's just the first trimester. All this is to say that when people start dropping unsolicited advice on the two of you, she may not always be in the proper mental state to respond well. She may be the sweetest, most gracious woman in the world, but pregnancy is essentially life lived under duress. Surely there are times in life when a person handles unsolicited advice well, but pregnancy isn't guaranteed to be one of those. This is why it falls to you to be the one to handle the avalanche of advice.

> **Once a woman is pregnant, there is no malady short of death that will gain you any sympathy.**

Is your mental state better than your wife's? That is an entirely different question, but allow me to remind you of something from the previous chapter: It doesn't matter. Once a woman is pregnant, there is no malady short of death that will gain you any sympathy.[1] You may be a little under the weather or in a funk, but when that well-meaning person begins giving advice, it is your job to step up to the plate and take one for the team.

KEEPING YOUR COOL

Second, you are probably going to have to show some wisdom and self-control. I will admit that often when someone decides to corner me with unsolicited advice, my initial reaction is not always gracious and Spirit-filled. Pregnancy is stressful for everyone involved, especially if this isn't your first baby, so you may not always be in the best frame of mind to handle it either. I suggest planning ahead. Work out a contingency plan for when someone decides they know everything there is to know about being pregnant and raising a baby and you just can't deal with it. I suggest you and your wife work out an excuse to end the conversation, maybe by using a code word or a signal—something that tips you off that she needs an exit strategy.

Consider this example.

ELAINA SHARP CHIMES IN

[1] Again, what am I? The sympathy ogre? Don't answer that.

A very nice woman who has successfully raised 19 children, all while home-schooling and running her own organic, gluten-free, essential oil–driven dairy farm, approaches you at church. You are distracted and not paying attention. Let's say this is your first pregnancy, and because you are a man, what happens next takes you by surprise. First, this woman begins to tell your wife that she should eat only organic quinoa grown by elves in Rivendell and that not to do so is to put her health and, most importantly, the health of the baby at risk. Hopefully by now you are paying attention, because your wife needs you. If your wife seems to be under duress, if she is giving you a preordained signal like tugging on her ear, or if you notice that she is constantly clenching and unclenching her fists, it would be good for you to step in. Your wife is a soldier pinned down on the battlefield, and she needs extraction ASAP.

You can interrupt and say something like, "Honey, can you help me look for my sunglasses? I think I left them in the car." You can turn to the individual who has pinned her down and say, "I'm so helpless without my wife. I would forget my head if it wasn't attached to my body." The other woman will naturally agree and nod because she will think this confirms everything she suspects about you, her own husband, and the male gender in general. Yes, this makes you look like a moron to the other woman, but to your wife you will look like Superman. You saved the day![2]

TEAM RECRUITMENT

Third, you must realize at some point during your pregnancy that there are an awful lot of teams. Some teams are pregnancy specific, and some aren't. Here a brief list of teams you will probably encounter at some point during your pregnancy.

The "breastfeed them until they go to college" team. Okay, I'm exaggerating a little bit, but only a little. Considerable research suggests that breastfeeding is the preferable scenario for feeding the baby. As a parent, you have signed up to put another small human being's needs above your own, so that should be a major

---

ELAINA SHARP CHIMES IN

[2] Or at least you saved her from unleashing holy you-know-what, which may or may not have resulted in your wife's incarceration.

factor in your decision-making process. Still, there are several reasons a woman might not breastfeed, and it really isn't anybody else's business anyway. Not everyone is as understanding of that as they should be, particularly when they are talking with a pregnant woman. As a rule, this team believes that if a baby cries, he or she needs Mama. Just remember that when people give you advice, sometimes it is perfectly appropriate to smile, nod, and then go do whatever you think is right. This is one of those times.[3]

The "baby must be on a schedule" team. As you might guess, this team is essentially mortal enemies with the breastfeed until college team. This team is controversial and will give you loads of literature backing their view. They believe that kids these days are too soft because they are coddled from the moment they are born. They might proffer wisdom, like "We wouldn't have all these snowflakes running around if parents had just made them eat on a schedule." They will tell you that if your kid cries and you respond with cuddling and, God forbid, a feeding, you are raising a slacker at best and, at worst, a hardened criminal who can trace their life of crime back to how you reacted in those first three months.

> They will tell you that if your kid cries and you respond with cuddling and, God forbid, a feeding, you are raising a slacker at best and, at worst, a hardened criminal who can trace their life of crime back to how you reacted in the first three months.

The "organic" team. This team isn't exclusive to pregnancy, but once a woman is pregnant, these loyal fans come in waves. Be prepared for multitudes of people—some you know well and some you don't—commenting on your wife's diet

---

ELAINA SHARP CHIMES IN

[3] The way it generally worked for us was each tiny human wanted me more than Daddy until they were weaned. Then they mostly wanted Daddy. If any moms are reading this, *just go with it.* You may be tempted to pout that they don't want Mommy as much anymore, but you will see eventually this is a precious gift. For example, when they say, "I need to go potty. I want *Daddy* to take me!" Score one point for Mom.

and insinuating that everything she eats is awful. Unless she is subsisting on that Rivendell-grown quinoa. Then she is right as rain.[4]

The "put headphones on a pregnant woman's belly and play classical music" team. This team espouses the idea commonly known as the "Mozart effect," which is the belief that classical music can and will improve IQ and academic performance in adults, children, and yes, even in babies in the womb. A lot of things about pregnancy make a woman feel awkward and rather silly, and unfortunately most of those are unavoidable. What is avoidable is putting headphones on your belly in the hopes that Mozart will somehow magically turn the baby inside you into a child prodigy. There is very little evidence this helps children and adults and no evidence this does anything positive at all for babies. But I guess if it makes a pregnant woman feel better, then who am I to argue?[5] Just know that if your kid struggles with long division, it probably isn't because you went easy on the Chopin in the womb.

> **If your kid struggles with long division, it probably isn't because you went easy on the Chopin in the womb.**

While I do not personally see any reason to endorse the headphones on the belly, one thing that I do heartily approve of is Daddy having long, meaningful talks with the baby in utero. One of my favorite things to do while Wonder Woman was pregnant was to get right up next to her belly and to talk to the baby. Sometimes I would tell the baby stories, sometimes I would explain things to the baby about life on the outside, and sometimes I would just tell the baby information I thought he or she should know (like our family roots for the St. Louis Cardinals but never the Chicago Cubs). The things dads have to say to their kids are a lot more interesting than Mozart.

Now that you are prepped for unsolicited advice, we come to a part of pregnancy that is as fun as it is stressful—naming your little bundle of joy.

ELAINA SHARP CHIMES IN

[4] Yum, lembas bread.

[5] I couldn't stand for anything to be remotely tight on my baby belly. It felt claustrophobic!

NAMING THE BABY

If making a baby tends to bring couples closer, then naming said baby can be the wedge that drives a couple apart. If this is you, don't worry; you are not alone. Fights over baby names are common, and with any luck, unlike John the Baptist's father, Zacharias, you won't be rendered unable to speak for the duration of the pregnancy.

> **Fights over baby names are common, and with any luck, unlike John the Baptist's father, Zacharias, you won't be rendered unable to speak for the duration of the pregnancy.**

Naming the baby doesn't have to be an issue, and it isn't for some couples. But for many, choosing a name for their child is a lot like navigating a minefield with a partner who can't decide whether they want you to survive. It probably isn't that dramatic, but naming a baby can make people touchy for a number of reasons.

FAMILY EXPECTATIONS

Extended family members' expectations factor into the decision. It's hard to overstate how important this is in some families. When grandparents expect a junior, or a third, or even a fourth, it puts a lot of pressure on a couple. If a woman marries a man with a III after his name, I have to think she assumed their firstborn son would be a IV, but perhaps I am wrong. If this is you and you are shocked, I am sorry for your struggle, but you really should have seen this coming.

When my parents were naming me, there was a small controversy over the name. Forty-one years later, my parents still give different answers as to the depth of the controversy. The joke is that I ended up with the name Aaron because it was the first one my dad saw in the baby name book. My middle name, Eugene, I inherited from my paternal grandfather, but my other grandfather's middle name was Gene, so I think they considered it something of a two-for-one special. Just know that if you name your firstborn son after one grandfather, there is a distinct possibility you are going to have to keep having kids until the other grandfather gets a child named after him as well. One of the reasons we didn't incorporate family names is that we felt like if we did so for the first kid, we would have to have at least two boys and two girls to cover everyone. But we are also now raising two boys and two girls, so what do I know?

THE NAMING RACE

Do you know about the race to get to the good names before all your friends use them up? When we first started talking seriously about trying to get pregnant, Wonder Woman liked several girl names. (Take note—they almost always have a list of several names. Many women have had the list since junior high.) Then friends of ours announced that they were having a baby girl and that her name would be the same as my wife's top choice. At the time it was disappointing to Wonder Woman, but by the time God gave us the Ballerina a few years later, we had warmed up to a different name, and all was well.

When you pick out a name or a pool of names from which to choose, you'll face the difficult task of making sure none of the names have any bad connotations for either of you. This might be harder than you expect. Part of the challenge is that you must factor in all the derivatives of a name. When you are talking about Michael, you also have to consider Mike. Anthony could become Tony. William could become Bill. Your wife may like the name Alexander, but if the kid in elementary school who pointed out to the whole class that you had a big nose was named Alex, this may be off the table. The truth is that once a child is named, that name is out there in the wild, and there is nothing you can do about what happens to it.

OVERTHINKING IT

I remember when a good friend from high school called to tell me that his wife was pregnant with their first child, a boy. He said, "His name is Gabriel, but he is going to go by Gabe." I remember thinking, "How do you know that? He might go by Gabe for the first few years of his life, but after that, isn't he going to be making that call?" You have to factor in an awful lot of variables here. Trust me, you don't want to be that parent constantly following your child around to correct everyone by telling them, "It's Jeff, not Jeffrey." I am telling you this for your own good.

It is possible to overthink baby names and get a little too cute. Now, this is a personal preference, so take it for what it's worth, but it has gotten more and more popular to put some crazy spin on your kid's name so that it's unique. You might be considering the name John, but instead of spelling it John or even Jon, you might decide to use a "u" instead of an "o" or maybe go real old-school European and spell it Jan but tell people it is pronounced "Yan." You might even be considering some sort of twist by using a dash or an apostrophe in there somewhere. Or perhaps you are planning on getting all your kids' names from the Old Testament prophets. Be unique if that's your bag, but for the sake of your child and all their future teachers, don't go off the deep end. No kid wants to spend the rest of their life explaining their name just because their parents couldn't help themselves.

Keep in mind that you have no idea what your kid is going to think about his or her name, and you have no idea what will happen culturally that will impact this decision. If you are my age and your parents named you Newman, you've probably heard people use your name derogatorily for years after the TV show *Seinfeld* was on the air. I've been impacted by a viral video of a skit by the comedy team Key and Peele. A teacher calls out a student named Aaron by saying, "You done messed up, A-A-Ron." I am called "A-A-Ron" no fewer than 25 times a week, and the video came out six years ago. I generally find this funny. My wife even bought a T-shirt with "You done messed up, A-A-Ron" on it. I'm not saying you should aim for boring, but the more unique your kid's name, the better the chances that he or she will be identified with something you never saw coming. The odds are that the names John and Betty aren't going to be ruined anytime soon.

> I'm not saying you should aim for boring, but the more unique your kid's name, the better the chances that he or she will be identified with something you never saw coming.

TILL DEATH OR BABY NAMES DO US PART

Adding to the challenge of this decision is the fact that you and your wife must agree on at least a first name and probably a middle name as well. You love each other, you have pledged before God to be committed to one another until death do you part, and you have even made a baby together. But something about settling on the name of the baby you two have created can be all but impossible.

A good friend of mine we will call Rodney (because that is his name) has been married to his long-suffering wife, Jody, for almost 30 years now. Their first two kids are twin girls. They got pregnant again less than a year after the first pregnancy, and for some reason, they just couldn't agree on a name for their firstborn son. Around and around they went until Rodney's wife went into labor. As they drove to the hospital with Jody in labor, the two began to argue over a name for the child who was about to be born. If you've never been through a pregnancy, this seems completely insane. If you've been through a pregnancy, you're probably thinking, "Of course they did!" Rodney and Jody both had a list of names, and they even agreed on some of the names, but not on their top choice.

The argument escalated all the way to the hospital until finally, in exasperation, Jody said, "Fine, we will name him Caleb!" a name on both of their lists but neither of their top choices. I've questioned Rodney's sanity on several occasions, but perhaps never as much as when he tells this story. I'm pretty sure that arguing with a pregnant woman about a baby name while she is in labor on the way to the hospital would be considered a justifiable reason for homicide in many countries. I know for sure that no woman on a jury who had been through childbirth would vote to convict that woman.

As many students of the Bible will tell you, names are very important in the Bible. Frequently the characters who grace the Bible's pages live up to their names—or in some cases, down to them. I can only speak to the Sharp family's quartet of small humans, but I see some evidence for this in our family as well. The child whose name means "grace" loves beauty. The child whose name means "life" is so full of life that many days we wish we would have named her something that meant "peace" or "tranquility."

I don't think a child's name is their destiny, but I do think there is something to parents being intentional about what a child is going to be called for the rest of his or her life. At the very least, if you name a child Nabal and he turns out not to be the brightest bulb in the box, you should have known better.

> At the very least, if you name a child Nabal and he turns out to not be the brightest bulb in the box, you should have known better.

Now that you've successfully tackled naming your offspring, it's probably time we had a frank conversation about how pregnancy and childbirth are portrayed in popular books, TV shows, and movies.

19

PREGNANCY IN POPULAR CULTURE

Making a baby and having a baby are nothing like they are portrayed in popular entertainment. Odds are that if you've watched a TV show or a movie with a pregnancy in it, you've seen a pregnancy myth or two on screen. If there is one thing producers and directors love, it is a good pregnancy plot, but like all things on the big and small screens, "based on a true story" allows for an awful lot of creative interpretations of reality. To help you be as ready for the real deal as possible, this chapter debunks seven myths about pregnancy you've probably seen in popular culture. And just to be fair, it also lists one thing popular depictions get (mostly) right.

> Odds are that if you've watched a TV show or a movie with a pregnancy in it, you've seen a pregnancy myth or two on screen.

MYTH #1

A woman's water breaks, and moments later a new baby has entered the world.

The truth is that labor can go quickly, but the process of a baby leaving the womb can also last a long, long time, particularly if it is a woman's first pregnancy.

If you have seen pregnancy represented in, for example, a sitcom, a woman is usually going about her business when suddenly her water breaks and there is a flood of water everywhere. Her husband then panics because he is an absolute imbecile incapable of walking and chewing gum at the same time. Within 10 minutes she is screaming in pain, cursing her pathetic excuse of a husband (who is still trying to find his car keys), and wondering why pregnancy was a good idea. Ten minutes later, the moron husband has finally gotten his wife into the car, but he has probably gotten lost on the way to the hospital. Finally, within 30 minutes of her water breaking, the couple rushes into the hospital with just enough time for the still-screaming woman to lie down as the baby emerges from her body. The husband, who got turned around in the hospital, makes it to the delivery room just in time to pass out.

With our first baby, Wonder Woman's water broke unexpectedly around six one morning. What followed was not a hurried rush to the hospital but a leisurely trip. We showered, double-checked our bags, made the appropriate calls, and eventually headed to the hospital.[1] That night, 16 hours later, our Zoologist was born. With each baby, labor went quicker, but just know there are plenty of times when things move at less than breakneck speed. You may be the couple who almost delivers in a car,[2] but the odds are you will not be.

MYTH #2

A pregnant woman has the strength of ten men and can crush her husband's hand during a contraction the same way King Kong crushes anything in his way.

Generally, this is depicted by a very small, petite woman who is married to a big, burly hulk of a man. A contraction hits, and she rips his arm off and begins beating him with it. This whole trope[3] is a blatant falsehood. Simply put, it is totally inconceivable that a pregnant woman's strength is that of 10 men. There is no way it is less than the strength of 20 men.

ELAINA SHARP CHIMES IN

[1] Via Starbucks, of course.

[2] *My worst nightmare!*

[3] I have a pretty good vocabulary, but I still had to look this one up. For those wondering, a *trope* is "a commonly recurring literary and rhetorical device, motif, or cliché" (per Wikipedia).

> It is totally inconceivable that a pregnant woman's strength is that of 10 men. There is no way it is less than the strength of 20 men.

MYTH #3

Babies come out of the womb relatively clean, they cry for a second, they are wrapped up in a blanket, and then they cuddle with their mother and pose for pictures with extended family.

First, babies do not come out of the womb clean. In fact, the whole process is rather messy. Going into my wife's first delivery, I didn't know how I would react.[4] I didn't think I would pass out in the delivery room, but I wasn't 100 percent sure. (After all, I did nearly pass out when they took us to the blood bank on an elementary school field trip to the hospital.) But I handled all the blood, fluids, and smells quite well.

Second, two of our four kids had short stays in the delivery room, so cuddle and picture time isn't always possible either. The Zoologist and the Ballerina both were whisked away rather quickly so a NICU doctor could start taking care of them immediately. Wonder Woman had been very explicit with me on the way to the hospital that no matter what happened to her in the delivery room, my job was to go with the baby and stay by his side. She said she would be surrounded by family, and my job was to accompany the baby to the nursery or wherever he went.

The Zoologist was born and quickly taken to the nursery, and then a nice doctor came up to me and introduced himself. He explained that our baby, who was what nurses call a "wimpy white boy"—seriously, this is an expression in the medical community—would need to spend some time in the NICU. While I was speaking with him, my brothers- and sisters-in-law were lurking nearby, listening in. After talking with the doctor, I turned and told them that Wonder Woman had given me marching orders, that I was following the baby to the NICU, and that one of them would need to explain to her what was going on. I might have

---

ELAINA SHARP CHIMES IN

[4] Especially since you almost passed out that one time when I was getting an IV put in.

had more luck getting one of them to volunteer to lick an Ebola lollipop, but at this point, I washed my hands of everything and did what I was told. When they took the Zoologist from the nursery to the NICU, I went with him, leaving them to sort it out.

> I might have had more luck getting one of them to volunteer to lick an Ebola lollipop, but at this point, I washed my hands of everything and did what I was told.

These are the things they don't show you on TV.

MYTH #4

Spicy food can induce labor.

You've already figured out that one of our main food groups, particularly during a pregnancy, is Mexican food. If there was a diet that was sure to induce an early labor, it would be the Sharp family's. Come to think of it, our first baby barely made it past 36 weeks, and none of them made it past 38. Actually, forget I said anything about this. Doctors will tell you this isn't true, but what do they know?

MYTH #5

Pregnant women consume approximately 18,000 calories a day because they are eating for two.

> If the woman wants to eat the white chocolate cheesecake with the Oreo crust, get her the white chocolate cheesecake with the Oreo crust. There are certain things that should be left to a woman and her OB/GYN.

In truth, medical professionals will tell you that a pregnant woman only needs to consume an average of 300 extra calories a day to provide the baby growing in her womb the sustenance it needs. Do I suggest to expectant fathers that they bring up this helpful little trivia tidbit to their wives? Never in a million years. If the woman wants to eat the white chocolate cheesecake with the Oreo crust, get her the white chocolate cheesecake with the Oreo crust. There are certain things that should be left to a woman and her OB/GYN.

MYTH #6

Pregnant women love to have their tummies rubbed by everyone, including casual acquaintances and complete strangers.

I'm not entirely sure why this seems like a good idea to people, but from what I have been able to gather through extensive research accumulated from pregnant women, this is almost universally loathed by women around the globe in the throes of pregnancy. I'm still trying to figure this out. Do people think a pregnant belly is like a magic lamp, and if you rub it, a genie comes out? Whatever the motivation, let me tell you that no matter what you see or hear, the pregnant woman in your life most likely hates this with a white-hot passion.[5]

MYTH #7

Women never take any sort of pain medication when they give birth. Popular depictions of pregnancies prove this is true.

I understand there are frequent skirmishes between team "natural birth" and team "give me the drugs," but according to popular culture, everyone is apparently giving birth in a very natural and excruciatingly painful manner. Let me be clear— I am not suggesting an epidural makes giving birth a walk in the park or anything resembling a pleasant experience.[6] I'm just saying that if you base your opinion on what you see represented on the screen, you might be inclined to assume that giving birth is probably a violation of the Geneva Convention.

ELAINA SHARP CHIMES IN

[5] Foolproof method of getting them to stop: Rub their belly too! That sweet, advice-giving older woman in your church will drop her hand off your belly like you've got leprosy.

[6] I may or may not have started asking my doctor for an epidural around week 30. I mean, that baby was getting big, and my back was hurting. Help a pregnant mama out!

> I'm just saying that if you base your opinion on what you see represented on the screen, you might be inclined to assume that giving birth is probably a violation of the Geneva Convention.

TRUTH #1

Though popular depictions of pregnancy have often missed the mark, they usually get this one right: A pregnant woman is prone to wild temperature swings and may run the air conditioner more than you thought was possible. It could be 105 degrees outside in the middle of July, but inside a pregnant woman's home, the average temperature is likely to be a chilly 47 degrees.[7] This is a part of that whole "babies are expensive" thing. You just never anticipated your electric bill to triple when your wife got pregnant. Surprise!

Now that we've covered popular myths about pregnancy, we are getting closer and closer to the delivery. Next let's look at contractions and false labor.

ELAINA SHARP CHIMES IN

[7] We live in Texas. You can always warm up by putting on more clothes, but it can get very awkward when a pregnant woman starts taking off her clothes.

20

FALSE LABOR AND CONTRACTIONS

As you have no doubt ascertained by this point in the book, I knew very little about pregnancy before Wonder Woman and I found out she was expecting for the first time. I'm an only child, and too much of my understanding of the process was probably influenced by TV, movies, and urban legends.

WHAT IS A CONTRACTION?

> One of the things that was news to me about pregnancy was that contractions don't necessarily mean "The baby is on the way, run for your lives!"

One of the things that was news to me about pregnancy was that contractions don't necessarily mean "The baby is on the way, run for your lives!" I felt pretty stupid when I learned that—until I did a little reading on the subject and realized that for most of human history, nobody else really understood contractions either. It wasn't until 1872 that a doctor by the name of John Braxton Hicks discovered contractions can begin as early as the second trimester. Dr. Hicks discovered that in the lead-up to the birth of a child, a woman's body practices to get ready for the big day. The birth is the Super Bowl, and the last few months are like the two weeks prior, when both teams practice like crazy (except there is no intermission with an overrated musical act). To undertake all this practice,[1] the muscles of a woman's uterus (the fact that we made it this far into the book without using the word "uterus" is a small miracle) tighten for a few seconds or perhaps as long as two minutes. As a guy, you cannot fathom this. Just follow the basic rule of thinking about pregnancy as a man and assume it is more pain than you can endure. God has blessed you by not making this part of manhood.[2]

There are a lot of factors that determine how many Braxton Hicks contractions a woman has, how early they start, and how intense they are. The fact that they can occur for three months can be a little disconcerting to a woman who has enough to deal with in life without her body turning the last three months of pregnancy into some strange version of spring training for her uterus. That's why at this stage in the pregnancy it's important for a husband to dial in, pay attention, and do what he can to help. You were warned.

PAYING ATTENTION

Before we get to what you can do to help, let's get to the paying attention part. Men have a well-earned reputation for not being terribly observant. The male gender means well, but keeping up with details, picking up on subtle clues, and noticing when the love of your life is grimacing in pain are not among our strong suits.[3] With that in mind, here are some things you might want to watch out for to tip you off that your wife is experiencing a contraction.

She lets out a verbal exclamation of some sort. This can take many forms. It might be a simple, one-syllable cry, such as "Ow!" or "Ouch!" or "Uggg!" or

---

ELAINA SHARP CHIMES IN

[1] Practice. We're talking about practice. We ain't talking about childbirth here, we are talking about practice. C'mon guys, aren't you impressed by my Allen Iverson impersonation?

[2] Actually, they have these simulations that allow men to experience pains very similar to contractions. Where do I sign you up?

[3] With our first baby, my Braxton Hicks contractions weren't terribly painful, but it did feel like our son was boxing in my belly. With my two girls, it felt like they were stretching spread-eagle inside my belly, with a hand in each side of my rib cage and their feet in my hips. I don't remember the fourth, probably because I was so busy chasing the other three around that I hardly noticed the Braxton Hicks contractions.

perhaps even "Oh wow!"[4] When you hear something like this, it would be good to put down the phone, mute the game, or pause whatever you are doing and check on your wife.

She suddenly grabs ahold of something with a grip so firm that it threatens to vaporize whatever she is holding. Perhaps the two of you are eating a meal, and for no apparent reason she grabs the table and holds on for dear life. Perhaps she randomly starts banging her fist on a wall or perhaps even your head. Or it could be that the two of you are sitting in church and suddenly she is clutching her Bible so firmly that you begin to wonder if she is undergoing an exorcism. This is just part of pregnancy, but the exorcism isn't far off.

Her face contorts, and she appears to no longer be breathing. One of the toughest things to do for any human being, male or female, is to breathe through pain. As a man, you've probably experienced this while enduring a tough workout, and for nine months your wife will be undergoing a tougher workout than anything you've ever done. When you see her face twist as if she was just zapped by a bolt of electricity, it's a good time to start paying attention. I know this is getting repetitive, but trust me. This is important.

> When you see her face twist as if she was just zapped by a bolt of electricity, it's a good time to start paying attention.

She does one or perhaps all these things and says, "Oh wow, there's a contraction!" Let me be clear: I don't think we men are all idiots. In general, the male species is far better than we get credit for in popular culture, but I'm trying to make things as plain as I can so you don't miss the point here. If she says she is having a contraction, you should trust her in this; she is going to know better than you what a contraction feels like. It doesn't mean you need to rush to the hospital right away, but a little sympathy wouldn't hurt anything.

ELAINA SHARP CHIMES IN

[4] Even a simple groan, ladies. They'll be trained to notice everything pretty quickly.

HELPING OUT

As the person in the relationship who is not carrying the baby in your own body and thus not experiencing contractions, it can be difficult for a guy to know what to do to help. Once a dude starts paying attention, he can feel helpless because the male gender tends to want to fix things. This is a quandary for a man whose wife is pregnant and really for marriage in general. Men are by nature fixers. When we hear of a problem, we like to present solutions. This is good when the problem is a dead car battery, but most of the time when our wives present a problem to us, it isn't a dead battery. Usually it is something about her feelings, and no matter how hard we try, this just isn't our forte. And by "not our forte," I mean that we men tend to define a problem and try to give our wives a solution, but by the time we are done, we have exacerbated the problem and added a couple more to it.

If you are going to truly help your wife, especially if she is pregnant and dealing with contractions, you are going to have to develop an ability that may not come naturally—the ability to empathize.

Every scientific study about empathy seems to confirm what God's Word said a long time ago. In several places, the Bible encourages and even commands empathy from followers of Christ. For example, Romans 12:15 says, "Rejoice with those who rejoice, and weep with those who weep" (NASB). This isn't an unusual sentiment on the pages of Scripture, but that doesn't necessarily mean it comes naturally.

> Your job when your wife is contracting—whether she is forgetting to breathe, her eyes are bulging out of her head, or she is crushing every small bone in your hand—is to empathize with her.

Your job when your wife is contracting—whether she is forgetting to breathe, her eyes are bulging out of her head, or she is crushing every small bone in your hand—is to empathize with her. Recently researchers at the University of Haifa in Israel conducted a study in which they measured what effect an empathetic partner had on someone in pain, including the pain of labor. They discovered that "the presence of partners during delivery is helpful in 60 percent of cases, suggesting that the partner's empathy and the quality of the birth interaction might explain the differences between the cases. Similarly, other studies showed that the father's presence increased positive experiences in all aspects of childbirth."[5]

Your wife's contractions will require your presence physically, mentally, and spiritually. Empathy can include a lot of things. It might mean paying more attention to your wife and less to a screen (let's be honest, you need to do this whether she is pregnant or not). It may mean listening to her tell you about the frustration of pregnancy without trying to fix it. And yes, it may mean holding her hand while she is contracting and praying that you will one day regain the use of that hand.

Rejoice with her when she rejoices, and weep with her when she weeps. Just be prepared to do a good bit more weeping than rejoicing. And make sure she keeps breathing when the contractions hit.

> **Rejoice with her when she rejoices, and weep with her when she weeps. Just be prepared to do a good bit more weeping than rejoicing.**

PUSH GIFTS

When contractions enter the picture, they should also serve as reminders that as a husband, you have some planning and shopping to do before the baby comes. It has become enormously popular in recent years for husbands to buy their wives "push gifts." There is a decent chance that the idea of a push gift is similar to nursery themes—an idea thought up by pregnant women who realize that no man in his right mind will argue with them. And if that is the case, they are right. Your wife may or may not be expecting a push gift, but if she is, when the contractions start to hit, it is time to get on the ball. If she isn't expecting one, take this as an opportunity to surprise her with thoughtfulness.[6]

ELAINA SHARP CHIMES IN

[5] Pavel Goldstein, "Holding Your Partner's Hand Can Ease Their Pain," *Aeon*, January 16, 2018, https://aeon.co/ideas/what-is-the-physiological-basis-of-the-healing-touch.
[6] Win-win.

For my wife's first two pregnancies, I tried to be ready with push gifts. But after that, things got so complicated just dealing with pregnancy that I fell down on the job. At some point, taking care of the children we already had consumed my life when Wonder Woman was pregnant. The one thing we did with every pregnancy was to have a celebratory dessert in the hospital. This was a tradition we never failed to keep. There is a restaurant not too far from the hospital that serves a bananas Foster cake.[7] Wonder Woman loves it, and so with every pregnancy while she was in the hospital, I would place a to-go order for this dessert and pick it up for her to eat as a special treat in her hospital room. Just trust me on this. You need to think this through beforehand. Once the baby is born, you can't expect to have your wits about you. Frankly, you will probably never have your wits about you again for the rest of your life the same way that you did before you became a father.

> Once the baby is born, you can't expect to have your wits about you. Frankly, you will probably never have your wits about you again for the rest of your life the same way that you did before you became a father.

Now that we've discussed contractions, it's time to think through a truly important and underrated part of pregnancy—packing for the hospital.

ELAINA SHARP CHIMES IN

[7] Can we have another baby so I can get that dessert again?

21

PACKING FOR THE HOSPITAL

When the due date draws near—or to be safe, even before it draws near—it will be time to pack a go bag for the hospital. If a pregnant woman is nervous about having to rush out of the house to go to the hospital at a moment's notice, she may strongly request her husband to pack for the hospital.[1] There's a good chance this request will be made far earlier than a husband believes is necessary, probably sometime in the first trimester. If this isn't the couple's first baby, the husband may ignore this wise counsel from his pregnant better half, believing he has all the time in the world to prepare. Bear in mind I speak from experience when I say this: Don't be that guy.[2]

Once you have packed your go bag for the hospital, consider keeping it in your car rather than in the house. If you are in a meeting at work on Wednesday morning and your wife calls to tell you she's in labor, the last thing you want to have to do is head home to get your bag. If she's at home, you can go get her and your bag, and all is well. But in case you haven't picked up on this, let me be clear: Very few times in pregnancy will you think to yourself, "Boy, that worked out perfectly, just like I planned." A more likely scenario is that your wife is at her work or anywhere other than home, and now you, dear husband, will have to go get her or meet her at the hospital.

ELAINA SHARP CHIMES IN

[1] This sounds familiar.

[2] You mean like the time my water broke at 36 weeks and you had nothing packed? Nada. Zip. Zilch.

> Very few times in pregnancy will you think to yourself, "Boy, that worked out perfectly, just like I planned."

Did I follow this advice? No. I am urging you to do something I never did. Does this make me a hypocrite? Probably. But that doesn't mean the advice isn't good. Besides, the poor woman can't even see her feet when she looks down at this point, so just do it.

Part of the reason men don't pack for the hospital as early as they should is that men think, "It's packing. I've packed before. As a matter of fact, I am a world champion packer. I can pack the trunk so well that if there were an Olympics for packing, I would have more gold medals than Michael Phelps." This is faulty thinking. Do not be deceived into thinking that packing for the hospital is the same as packing for a family vacation. Specific items must be packed. None of this is life and death, but trust me when I tell you it is better to be overpacked than underprepared. Here are four must-have, do-not-forget, turn-the-car-around-even-though-your-wife-is-in-labor items necessary for your trip to the hospital. (Okay, don't turn the car around. That would be foolish and possibly suicidal.)

1. The best camera you own (which may or may not be your phone).

> There were no photos of a minutes-old Aaron screaming because no one was even present in the room to do the photographing. We have more photos of each of our children's births than my parents have of the first 18 years of my life.

True story: When I was born, my poor mother was in the delivery room by herself. My father and my grandmother both bailed on the process. This probably says a lot about why I am the way I am. How I've managed to make it this far in life without serious therapy is a great mystery. Also, the fact that my mom did not spend years working through her anger and bitterness at her husband and mother says a lot about my mom. There were no photos of a minutes-old Aaron scream-ing because no one was even present in the room to do the photographing. We have more photos of each of our children's births than my parents have of the first 18 years of my life. Welcome to life in the twenty-first century, where things like rolls of film and paying for film to be developed are relics of a bygone era, much like rotary phones and civil discourse.

2. Every electrical device charger you own.

Phones, tablets, computers, and whatever other electronic devices you may have will probably be in full use at the hospital. Labor may last quite a while, and before it's all said and done, you may spend a lot of time waiting. You will proba-bly be texting, FaceTiming, and posting to social media more photos, videos, and updates than you can possibly imagine.[3] Make sure you can charge everything you need. It wouldn't be a bad idea to have a couple of extension cords and power strips handy as well. If you have access to a generator, you might want to keep it on standby too.

3. Bite-size food of some sort.

Here's one thing nobody talks about: Once the festivities begin, your wife won't be able to eat, but there is a 99 percent chance she will be hungry, and ice chips can only take a person so far.

> Also, to eat in front of a hungry woman who is in labor is to behave reck-lessly with your own safety and well-being.

In a later chapter, I'll get into specifics about a husband's dietary concerns dur-ing delivery, but just know that snacks small enough to be hidden can be real life-savers for the dad-to-be. The last thing your wife needs while she is in the often

---

ELAINA SHARP CHIMES IN

[3] That is, until your sweet wife looks at you and with the utmost kindness says, "Honey, could you please put your phone away so you can hold my leg while I push?" Not that I know from experience, of course.

long and painful process of pushing a live human being out of her body is to deal with a hangry husband who is on the verge of passing out because he hasn't gotten enough to eat. Also, to eat in front of a hungry woman who is in labor is to behave recklessly with your own safety and well-being. If nothing else, keep a bunch of bite-size candy bars in a bag, sneak them into your pockets, and step out into the hallway for a minute to throw them down your throat. You'll stave off hunger without making things tougher for your wife, and you'll get a chance to apply Proverbs 9:17 (NIV): "Food eaten in secret is delicious!" (This was a test. That verse is ripped completely out of context. It's not encouraging you to eat Snickers bars in the hallway of the hospital. If you read that and thought, "Yeah, the Bible says it," put this book down and spend some time in Bible study right now! But even though Solomon didn't say anything about it, were he here today, I think he would agree with the advice just the same.)

4. A sweatshirt, a jacket, a blanket, a fire-starter kit, and possibly an industrial-size space heater.

> Assume any time you spend in the hospital will be roughly equivalent to camping in Antarctica, and you will be on the right track.

Hospitals tend to be cold, and a woman's hormones on delivery day can cause her internal thermostat to perform amazing tricks. Assume any time you spend in the hospital will be roughly equivalent to camping in Antarctica, and you will be on the right track.[4]

I must offer a disclaimer at the end of this chapter because a lot of people don't go to the hospital to deliver their babies. More than a few people now choose to

---

ELAINA SHARP CHIMES IN

[4] Two words: night sweats.

have their babies at home or at a birthing center. Since this is not the route we chose, I can't speak authoritatively or from experience about what you need to pack for these circumstances. It would seem to me, however, that packing for a birthing center is much like packing for the hospital except you have to factor the lack of a cafeteria into your plans. And one of the brilliant features of an at-home birth is that this entire chapter has been completely pointless for you. You don't have to pack your camera; when you need it, you just go to the next room to get it. It might also be easier to sneak some snacks at home as well, but don't base your decision purely on that.

Since we have now discussed packing for the hospital, it is time to talk about the trip to the hospital with a woman in labor.

UNEXPECTED LABOR

For thousands of years of human existence, all labor was essentially unexpected. The modern world, however, has seen the advent of scheduled deliveries. We take certain things for granted, like due dates, which would have been seen in the ancient world as a message from God. Think about it—a woman has a positive pregnancy test, goes to see her doctor, and has the pregnancy confirmed. The doctor and the woman chat about periods and other details that most men do their best to tune out, and then the doctor runs the numbers and gives you an expected due date.

DUE DATES

> We never had a child even remotely close to the due date, but then, our children are all rather contrarian in their own ways.

It is important to remember that dates are sort of ballpark figures. We never had a child even remotely close to the due date, but then, our children are all rather contrarian in their own ways. I'm not sure where they get it from. Still, the idea that you could look at a calendar and have even a rough estimate is probably something that would have made biblical women like Sarah or Mary green with envy. Yes, they had a pretty good idea of how long a pregnancy lasted, so it wasn't like a woman just went into labor one day with no idea that she was pregnant. But still, having more information must be better, right? And of course, scheduled deliveries are on another level altogether.

Most scheduled deliveries are scheduled inductions or scheduled Cesarean sections (typically referred to as C-sections). Three of my wife's four deliveries were induced, so only 25 percent of the Sharp births included what I am calling unexpected labor. This isn't to say that Wonder Woman wasn't stressing over the possibility of going into labor unexpectedly with each child, because she most definitely was.

A few years ago, a viral video showed a man driving his very-much-in-labor wife to the hospital. As the video progresses, it becomes clear that they aren't going to make it to the hospital, and before you know it, she has delivered a baby in the car, all while her husband is driving to the hospital and somehow, for some unconscionable reason, filming the whole debacle with his phone.[1] We were in the midst of pregnancy number two or number three when this video came out, and for a time it was all my wife could think about. Repeatedly she forced me to swear I would do everything in my power, including breaking every traffic law on the books in the great state of Texas, to ensure she did not give birth in the car. She also threatened my life if I ever filmed her in labor in the car.

> **At no point in married life, before or after having become a father, would it have occurred to me to whip out my phone to document my wife delivering a baby in the car while I was driving down the road.**

To be clear, this was an unnecessary threat. At no point in married life, before or after having become a father, would it have occurred to me to whip out my phone to document my wife delivering a baby in the car while I was driving down the road.[2] The fact that someone thought this was a good idea leaves me a little speechless.

Wonder Woman was especially nervous about where and when she would go

---

ELAINA SHARP CHIMES IN

[1] *He filmed the whole thing. While driving.*

[2] This is one of the many reasons why I love you.

into labor with baby number four. Her labor was quicker with each delivery, so by the time we reached number four, we wondered if it would be more like a drive-thru than a fine dining experience. She was nervous that either she would give birth in the car[3] or her water would break at work[4] and she would have to get from her workplace to the hospital while in labor. She works with her dad, so I didn't think this was as big a worry as she did, but thankfully for us, this didn't end up being an issue.

WHAT YOU CAN'T CONTROL

Pregnancy is a brilliant example of why the Scriptures caution us about worry. Take Paul's famous admonition in Philippians 4:6-7: "Be anxious for nothing, but in everything by prayer and supplication, with thanksgiving, let your requests be made known to God; and the peace of God, which surpasses all understanding, will guard your hearts and minds through Christ Jesus" (NKJV). These are fantastic, wonderful verses. They aren't complicated to understand, but many times they can be hard to apply. I think one of the most difficult parts of pregnancy has to be the expectant parents' lack of control. For nine months, anything can go wrong at any time, and then you hit a certain point in the pregnancy at which if anything goes wrong, or if anything goes right, you might be rushing to the hospital.

> I feel rather lucky that in four pregnancies, we only had one trip to the hospital for false labor. This was when we were expecting the Jedi. Looking back on it, we should have realized this child was going to be a handful.

The best part about all this is that you might grab your bags and rush to the hospital only to be told to return home because it was false labor. I feel rather lucky that in four pregnancies, we only had one trip to the hospital for false labor.[5] This

---

ELAINA SHARP CHIMES IN

[3] Very, very bad.

[4] Even worse.

[5] Actually, I was in real labor. But I was also very dehydrated. So as soon as they gave me fluids, the contractions stopped.

was when we were expecting the Jedi. Looking back on it, we should have realized this child was going to be a handful.

"MY" EXPERIENCE

Perhaps this would be a good time to discuss a delivery that is near and dear to my heart—my own. I was present for these events but have no firsthand knowledge of them, having been in the womb and all.

It was a lovely spring Monday in West Texas. (That's "west" as in the opposite of east, not to be confused with the town of West, Texas, which is ironically located in the eastern half of the state.) My mother was 22 years young, had been married for four years and pregnant for nine months, and unbeknownst to her, had been in labor since the night before.

That morning, my mom gritted her teeth through what she thought was just some significant back pain brought on by carrying around a growing human being in her body for nine long months (she was also past her due date). She told my dad good-bye as he headed off to work, and then she spent the first part of the morning trying to clean the house. Yes, she really did try to clean the house. She was in enough pain that the average person would have committed a homicide for pain pills, but she got out the vacuum and away she went.

> She was in enough pain that the average person would have committed a homicide for pain pills, but she got out the vacuum and away she went.

While my mom was attempting to clean the house, my dad was working as the principal of a Christian school. Today, Christian schools are a common thing, but this school was the first of its kind in the area. There were all sorts of problems, as is common with something new and innovative. Questions such as "Do we accept kids who were kicked out of public schools?" and "What do we do when a student never shows up for school?" that no one had ever considered were par for the course. On this Monday, the schedule included a chapel service, which my dad was in charge of.

At some point while the students and teachers were in chapel, the school receptionist answered a phone call. On the other end of the phone was my now very-much-in-labor mother asking to speak to my dad. As the story goes, the conversation went something like this:

> MY IN-LABOR MOTHER: I need to speak with my husband.
>
> RECEPTIONIST: I'm sorry, he is in chapel and cannot be bothered.
>
> MY STILL-IN-LABOR MOTHER: Okay.

Now, I like words; I am an author, after all. I have a few pet peeves with words, and one of those has to do with the blatant and bordering-on-criminal misuse of the word "literally." People say things like "This iPhone update is literally the worst thing in history." Well, thank goodness those who lived through the Black Death did not have to update their smartphones. Or occasionally I will hear people get so offended they will say, "I am so mad I literally can't speak right now!" This is quite surprising, since there are words emerging from their mouths at that very moment. All this to say I do not use the word "literally" lightly. But in my four decades on this planet, I have never met another woman who would ever have just said, "Okay." My mom is, to the best of my knowledge, literally the only person on the planet who would have accepted that answer. Most of the women I know well would have reached through the phone, grabbed the receptionist by the throat, and explained to her that if she did not have my dad on the line in less than five seconds, the pregnant woman on the other end of the line would do unspeakable, painful things to her in such a manner that her ancestors, who had been in the grave for hundreds of years, would regret her foolishness. If you feel the need to poll women and see if any of them would have reacted as my mom did, feel free. I have yet to find one.

The phone call now over and her attempts to clean now impossible in such pain, my mom lay down on the couch, which is where my dad found her when he came home midmorning to pick her up to take her to her regularly scheduled doctor's appointment. To his credit, my dad would have come running had he known of any phone calls, and at this juncture, he urged my mom to skip the doctor and just go to the hospital. My mom, however, refused. She did not want to go to the hospital unless she was really in labor, largely because they didn't have a lot of money, and she was trying to make sure she only paid for one hospital visit.

Off they went to the doctor's office. They had only been there a few moments when the doctor said, "You need to go to the hospital." Thankfully, my dad had the good sense not to gloat and say, "I told you so." How do I know he didn't do that? I know because he lived long enough to meet me. In fact, I just spoke with him last night. Mouth off to a woman in labor, and your time on this planet is short.

> **Mouth off to a woman in labor, and your time on this planet is short.**

They left the doctor's office, and up to this point my dad had done pretty well, but that was all about to change. My dad decided that since the hospital was near the apartment complex my grandparents operated, he could take a little detour. My dad saw my grandfather mowing the apartment complex lawn, pulled up with my mom groaning and gripping the car's armrests, and yelled out the window, "Hey, Dad, we're going to the hospital to have the baby!" Having been through this twice as a husband, my grandfather, known affectionately as Papaw Sharp, began frantically waving his hands and screaming, "Go on, boy! Go!" My dad heeded this fatherly advice and headed straight to the hospital without any further stops.

LESSONS FOR DAD

To summarize, here is what you need to focus on as your wife's pregnancy progresses.

First, be ready to go at a moment's notice. Second, do not video your pregnant wife in the car. Third, make sure your place of employment knows that your wife is pregnant and that if she calls the receptionist, there is *literally* nothing in the world that should keep her from transferring the call. Fourth, when driving the poor woman in labor, proceed straight to the hospital without taking any side trips.[6] That pretty much covers the basics.

Now that we have discussed unexpected labor, it's time to cover the other option—inductions.

ELAINA SHARP CHIMES IN
[6] Except Starbucks, of course.

INDUCTIONS

Between 20 and 40 percent of births are induced. There are several reasons a doctor may decide to kick-start the process. The doctor may be concerned about the health of the mom, the health of the baby, the pregnancy continuing past the due date, or the due date conflicting with the World Series. Just kidding about the World Series, but a hot debate is currently raging about inductions performed for nonmedical reasons. I have no intention of weighing in on that debate in this chapter. This is a decision that the woman, her husband, and her doctor should make. Being due during the World Series was just poor planning on your part.

> There are several reasons a doctor may decide to kick-start the process. The doctor may be concerned about the health of the mom, the health of the baby, the pregnancy continuing past the due date, or the due date conflicting with the World Series.

One word of caution about inductions: A person could be forgiven for assuming that an induction leads to a smooth and easy delivery. If you are that person, I hate to burst your bubble, but nothing in pregnancy is easy.

INDUCTIONS AND THE BEST-LAID PLANS

Our second pregnancy was our first induction. Wonder Woman had been on bed rest for a few weeks before the big day arrived. I spent the night in the hospital with her the night before, and the next morning we got up early to go to the delivery room. (Why are inductions always scheduled early in the morning?) We got settled in, some family arrived, and the medical team began the process of inducing labor. A few hours into things, there was some progress, but it was going rather slowly. Wonder Woman, her nurse, and the assembled family all thought it would be a good idea for me to make my way to the cafeteria to have a good lunch. Wonder Woman was surrounded by family, and we were easily hours away from a baby making an appearance. So with my wife's blessing (I can't stress this part enough), I made my way to the cafeteria for a nice meal.[1]

The hospital where we had our babies serves Chick-fil-A, so I honored God by having a sanctified chicken sandwich, and I distinctly remember thinking, "Today I am going to be a father for the second time. I should have some chocolate cake." I leisurely ate my chicken sandwich and waffle fries. This would be my last chance to breathe for a while, so I was in no hurry. Besides, it wasn't like I was needed in the labor and delivery room right now anyway. Finally, after ruminating over my chocolate cake, I eased over to the elevators and moseyed up to the room, ready for the long haul of labor. My belly was full, my taste buds were pleased, and I was ready to go welcome my first daughter into the world, no matter how long it took.

The elevator stopped on the labor and delivery floor, and I ambled past the empty nurse's station. As I came around the corner, I found all our family in the hallway. When they saw me, they all started pointing at the door and hollering that I'd better get in there. I may not be the brightest crayon in the box, but at this point, even I realized it was time to move a little quicker. I rushed into the room to find my wife emotional, upside down, and surrounded by many medical professionals scurrying around the room like mice smelling cheese but not finding it.

> I rushed into the room to find my wife emotional, upside down, and surrounded by many medical professionals scurrying around the room like mice smelling cheese but not finding it.

ELAINA SHARP CHIMES IN

[1] What happened to your bite-size sneaky snacks?

I ran to Wonder Woman's side to find out what in the world was going on. She grasped my hand, informing me that I was not allowed to leave the room again, and then I got an explanation about all the excitement. Not long after I left (probably about the time I was just relishing my first bite of my tasty chicken sandwich), nurses hurried into the room. They told the family to wait in the hallway, and they quickly turned Wonder Woman over on her other side and elevated her feet. One of the things that amazes me about doctors and nurses is how they can breeze around a room, working feverishly, and remain calm at the same time. Most of us don't have this ability. While they scrambled around the room, flipping my wife and turning her upside down, they explained that the baby's heart rate had suddenly plummeted and that they were afraid she had shifted and was lying on the umbilical cord. If changing my wife's position didn't increase the baby's heart rate, my wife would be immediately taken into an operating room for an emergency C-section.

> The woman's emotions before she is pregnant form the baseline, or as you will call it by the second trimester, "The time before the great storm."

As an aside here, based on my years as a husband, I've noticed that God made women different from men in many ways, and one of those ways has to do with the emotions. This isn't news to anyone, and we've already talked about it in a previous chapter. But it is important for a man married to a woman great with child to note there are increasing levels of emotion for a woman. The woman's emotions before she is pregnant form the baseline, or as you will call it by the second trimester, "The time before the great storm." Then come a woman's emotions when she is pregnant, which far surpass anything you have ever seen. Next are a woman's emotions when she is in labor, which make the dark clouds of the second trimester seem like a pleasant, sunshiny day. And finally, we have a woman in labor who just heard the doctor utter the phrase "emergency C-section." At this point, you must be there for your wife; you must be her rock, her Gibraltar. You cannot stand and tell the storm to be still like Jesus did, but you can sit by your wife and hold her while everyone rushes around her in a frenzied state. Plant yourself like an unmovable tree beside your wife because this is what a man does—and because she has a grip on your hand from which the Jaws of Life could not free you.

After just a few moments (by the time I had meandered up to the room, almost all the excitement was dying down[2]), we were told the baby's heartbeat had jumped back up to where it was supposed to be. The baby *had* been pressing on the umbilical cord, and when the team began to turn and twist Wonder Woman, the repositioning rectified the situation in the womb. We breathed a sigh of relief, and a few hours later, we welcomed our beautiful little Ballerina into the world.

INDUCTIONS AND PREGNANCY BRAIN

So our first induction was full of excitement. Our second induction was relatively devoid of drama, and the only problem with our third induction was our own inability to tell time like normal adult human beings. Wonder Woman understood from the hospital that we were supposed to call them at 4:00 a.m. to let them know we were on the way to make sure they had a room available, and then we were supposed to be there at 5:00 a.m. This meant we were going to be paying a babysitter to come to our house at 4:30 a.m., but you do what you have to, and we wanted family to be with us at the hospital, not home babysitting. We got up at 3:30 a.m. to start getting ready, and the very pregnant Mrs. Sharp called the hospital to confirm that we were on our way. However, when she was talking to the nurse, the nurse said we didn't actually have to be there until 7:00 a.m.

The problem was that the babysitter was already on the way. We couldn't very well tell someone who had gotten up at 3:00 a.m. to go back to her house and come back in a couple of hours, so we just left when she got there as if we had to go to the hospital immediately. Wonder Woman insisted that we stop and get me breakfast. I think she was still a little jumpy from the umbilical cord incident with the second baby. I thought this was a trick, so at first I refused, but finally I gave in, and we stopped to get me something to eat because my wife is a saint and a woman

---

ELAINA SHARP CHIMES IN

[2] Yeah, because you abandoned me for Chick-fil-A.

who is to be praised.[3] After I ate, we drove to the hospital, where we both napped in the car until it was time to go in.

Just remember, inductions may be planned, but we always do well to remember Proverbs 16:9—"We can make our plans, but the LORD determines our steps." It might also be a good idea to have both of you confirm what time you are supposed to be at the hospital before you secure a babysitter.

Now that we've discussed inductions, it's time to talk about the big event—labor.

ELAINA SHARP CHIMES IN

[3] Now I'm blushing. Keep going.

LABOR

It's go time. You are in the delivery room. This is happening. You are about to become parents. You are not prepared for what is about to happen. The dad is about to watch a baby emerge from his wife's body in a way that is simultaneously miraculous and horrifying. There is no going back. In a matter of hours, perhaps even minutes, your life will never be the same.

This will be one of the most amazing and memorable moments of your life. You will never forget this moment as long as you live. If you have several kids, there is a good chance you will lose your mind by your early forties and won't remember your own name, but this is something you will always remember.

> If you have several kids, there is a good chance you will lose your mind by your early forties and won't remember your own name, but this is something you will always remember.

Hopefully you have your camera (with a fully charged battery). Hopefully you have the appropriate smartphone devices (with fully charged batteries and charge cables). Hopefully you have managed to snack enough. Hopefully you got enough rest last night. Hopefully you aren't on the verge of passing out.

Here are a few items to remember as things get going.

THE CELL PHONE

First, if labor goes on for a while, a lot of people will be texting and messaging you, wanting to know what's happening. It's good to keep everyone informed, but know that as the labor gets more intense and the time to start pushing draws near, your wife will expect you to either put the phone down or be prepared to have it shoved down your throat. Or so I've heard.

THE CENTIMETERS

Second, you are going to hear a lot about centimeters. Ten is good, and it is the number your wife is aiming for. Centimeters are very important when it comes to the baby making his or her way out of the womb. At some point, you are going to be tempted to do math, perhaps even advanced geometry, but trust me when I tell you that this is a time for theology, not math. God designed childbirth to be an amazing and wonderful event that defies explanation. When you are tempted to put pen and slide rule to paper to run the numbers on how this all works, remember that this whole thing was designed by a God who loves you and who is sovereignly in control of all things, even centimeters.

> When you are tempted to put pen and slide rule to paper to run the numbers on how this all works, remember that this whole thing was designed by a God who loves you and who is sovereignly in control of all things, even centimeters.

THE MEANING OF "EFFACED"

Third, at some point, a doctor or a nurse is going to use the word "effaced," which is always accompanied by a percentage. A nurse will say "She is 60 percent effaced" or something like that. It is possible that a member of our extended family thought this term referred to how much of the baby's face was visible.[1] So if the

---

ELAINA SHARP CHIMES IN

[1] Easily one of my favorite memories of this family member.

woman in labor was 50 percent effaced, this person thought that meant you could see half of the baby's face. This is not even remotely what medical professionals mean when they talk about how much a woman in labor is effaced. What does "effaced" mean? This isn't a medical journal—ask an OB/GYN. I can't do everything for you.[2]

THE UNEXPECTED

Fourth, you should be prepared for anything to happen. Life can take crazy turns while a woman is pushing. Acquaintances who lived in Japan in 2011 tell the story of how the wife went into labor just as the tsunami struck the island. This may not happen to you. In fact, the odds are microscopic that it would. But if you have enough kids, something weird is bound to happen during labor. Do you remember the Bible verse that says, "All things must be done properly and in an orderly manner" (1 Corinthians 14:40 NASB)? That verse has nothing to do with labor and delivery.

During Wonder Woman's labor with our fourth baby, the Jedi, things went haywire. This is the one where we got up insanely (and unnecessarily) early to go to the hospital. With three kids already at home, we had a well-choreographed plan for making sure someone was watching the kids while we were at the hospital. We scheduled a babysitter for most of the day. If labor persisted into the late afternoon, we had good friends, both of whom are teachers and parents, who were going to hang out at the house until my parents could go get the kids after the baby was born.

Labor for the Jedi went a little longer than we had hoped, so our friends dutifully showed up at our house at the appointed time to keep an eye on our kiddos. For a while, everything went smoothly at the house and at the hospital. But this soon changed. Labor progressed…we were just moments away from clearing our family out of the delivery room so Wonder Woman could start to push…and I got a text from our friends.

Our little Ballerina, four years old at the time, had been running in the house

---

ELAINA SHARP CHIMES IN
[2] You still don't know, do you?

when she tripped and fell. This was not something especially noteworthy, as kids run and fall in our house dozens of times a day. This time, however, when she tripped, she fell headlong into the wooden rocking chair Wonder Woman gave me as a wedding present. A phone call ensued, they sent us pictures of the cut above her eye, and while my wife was rapidly approaching ten centimeters, we had to come up with a plan.

The consensus was that the cut was deep enough to send the Ballerina to a doctor. My sister-in-law, who is a labor and delivery nurse, would be given the honor and privilege of being the first one of our extended family to meet the Jedi. As soon as she had met her new nephew and gotten the requisite pictures (assuming he wasn't rushed off to the NICU), she would leave the hospital to take the Ballerina to an urgent care facility. My parents would still pick up the other two kids, and they could decide what to do from there. After we put all this together in a couple of minutes, we shooed family out of the room, and shortly we welcomed the Jedi into the world.

From there, things got really crazy. I will never forget the weather the day the Jedi was born—a torrential downpour.[3] Sometimes in Texas it rains like God forgot His promise to never flood the earth again, and this was one of those days. It mattered because it meant that everyone who was headed back to our house in a far-north suburb—my sister-in-law to get the Ballerina and my parents to get the Zoologist and the Fashionista—got stuck in awful Dallas traffic. The Ballerina's trip to the urgent care center was a bust because the cut was so close to her eye that the doctors sent them to a hospital emergency room. By the time it was all over, my sister-in-law ended up at Target buying pajamas and other necessities for the Ballerina so she could just spend the night at my in-law's house after the emergency room doctor used glue to seal the cut. We spent the first few moments of our young son's life getting to know him and coordinating his sister's first trip to the ER. At least we weren't in a tsunami.

ELAINA SHARP CHIMES IN

[3] I don't remember it raining. But then again, I wasn't outside much that day.

> We spent the first few moments of our young son's life getting to know him and coordinating his sister's first trip to the ER. At least we weren't in a tsunami.

THE BLOOD

Fifth, if you can't handle the sight of blood, this may be a rough experience for you. I was a little worried about that before our first baby. I've never been great with the sight of blood. I mentioned earlier that when I was in elementary school, we took a field trip to the hospital, where they took us to the blood bank. My dad, who was with us on this field trip, looked over and saw me getting woozy. He had to pick me up and carry me out of the room before I passed out. My concern about how I would handle the blood associated with delivery was not unwarranted.

I also already explained how I was told with every baby that if the baby leaves the delivery room, it is my job as a father who doesn't want to be murdered by his wife to stay by the baby's side no matter what happens. I have a distinct memory of walking out of the delivery room, following our tiny little boy's hospital bassinet, and looking back and thinking, "It looks like they filmed *Saving Private Ryan* in here."[4] It is not an exaggeration to say that a lot of labor ends with blood, guts, and body parts everywhere.

THE MESS

Sixth, newborn babies are very, very messy and dirty. The nurses will clean them up while they are weighing and measuring them, but just know that all these pictures you are taking are going to be of a messy child. Also, there is a decent chance that your baby may not look entirely like a human. Along with being covered in fluids and slime, a baby's head can be a little misshapen—or even a lot. Do not let this alarm you.

ELAINA SHARP CHIMES IN

[4] It's a wonder we had babies two, three, and four after that mental image.

THE UMBILICAL CORD

Seventh, cutting the umbilical cord is a weird thing. I'm not sure why this became a tradition, but here we are. All things considered, I wasn't especially interested in cutting the umbilical cord, but I knew Wonder Woman wanted me to, and if you get nothing else out of this book, remember that the job of a man married to a pregnant woman is to love her, honor her, cherish her, take care of her, and do whatever is necessary to keep her healthy and happy. So yeah, I cut all four of our kids' umbilical cords. It's weird because you are basically using scissors to cut something squishy. Just man up, cut the cord, and call it a day. If you made it through the delivery, this is nothing.

> It's weird because you are basically using scissors to cut something squishy. Just man up, cut the cord, and call it a day. If you made it through the delivery, this is nothing.

As an aside, perhaps my proudest "keeping my head about me in the delivery room" moment involved the umbilical cord. After 16 hours of labor, the time to greet our firstborn had arrived. The doctor said *push*, and Wonder Woman pushed. The Zoologist's head began to emerge, but the umbilical cord was wrapped around his neck. The doctor quickly said, "Okay, stop pushing," while she unwrapped the cord. Thankfully, I had enough sense *not* to look at my wife, who was squeezing my hand so tight that I never expected to get full range of motion back, and say, "Hey, honey, stop pushing. The cord is wrapped around his neck." Such a statement, while honest, would have no doubt inspired a woman in labor to push whether she meant to or not. I kept my mouth shut and proved I had at least a modicum of sense, even in the delivery room.

Now that we've discussed the actual event of the birth, it's time to move past the details to discuss the wonder of childbirth.

THE WONDER OF IT ALL

During a pregnancy and especially childbirth, you can easily become so consumed by everything going on that you miss the wonder and beauty of what is happening. Having a child is an overwhelming experience. It can be tense, nerve-racking, exhausting…and I hate to break it to you, but it gets worse after the baby is born. This is why it's so important for you to take a few moments to revel in the miracle of what is happening.

The best time to do this might be as the due date draws near, it might be in the delivery room before the big moment, or it might even be as you cast an awestruck gaze into the nursery where your newborn is swaddled and cooing. But whenever you do it, make sure to take the time to jot some things down or at least spend a few minutes lost in thought.

THE GIFT FROM GOD

God—the very God who made the universe, who hung the stars in the sky, who first spun the earth on its axis, who made the giraffe tall, who gave the zebra its stripes, who put the oceans in their place, who parted the Red Sea, who sent fire from heaven at Elijah's request, who sent His own Son to be born in a manger to save the world from sin—decreed that you (yes, you) would be the parent of this brand-new baby. On one hand, this is a very intimidating thought, but it should also be immensely comforting. This same God is sovereign over all creation. He does not make mistakes, and He declared that the privilege and challenge of raising this child were specifically for you.

> This same God is sovereign over all creation. He does not make mistakes, and He declared that the privilege and challenge of raising this child were specifically for you.

In case you doubt this is the case, think about this simple phrase in Psalm 127:3: "Children are a gift from the LORD." It's a simple phrase, but it packs a tremendous theological punch. For all the amazing science, kooky old-wives' tales, and superstitions that seem to hover like a deep fog around pregnancy, there is one simple, inescapable truth that Solomon (yes, this psalm was written by Solomon) wanted us to understand in Psalm 127—children are given to parents by God. It is not an accident that you are going to be a parent, and it is no accident you are going to be this particular child's parent. God always knows what He is doing. This child is a gift from a loving heavenly Father who always does what is best.

> It is not an accident that you are going to be a parent, and it is no accident you are going to be this particular child's parent. God always knows what He is doing.

It's easy to forget this simple theological truth later, like during the first few months. Our Zoologist was a shock to my system. He came early, spent a few days in the NICU, and then was very colicky when he came home from the hospital. His days and nights were messed up, and as an only child, he changed my life in ways that reverberated like an earthquake for weeks.

THE COMING STORM

We got into a rhythm in the first few weeks. Wonder Woman would go to bed early, and I would stay up to feed the baby a bottle at 11:00 p.m. Mama would get up and feed him at 2:00 a.m., and I would get up to feed him another bottle at 5:00 a.m. That way she got two solid blocks of sleep, and I got to sleep through the 2:00 a.m. feeding. At least that was how it was supposed to work. Because he was colicky, he tended to spit up a lot, which caused feedings that should have lasted a few minutes to drag on and on. At one ill-fated late-night feeding, I was burping him when he somehow managed to spit up and headbutt me in the nose at the same time. I exclaimed "Ow!" as a reflex, which startled him, causing him to recoil backward, taking a fistful of chest hair with him.[1] After this, I always fed my children with a shirt on.

The Zoologist also woke up angry. It was like he thought his hunger was a personal attack perpetrated on him by these two obviously incompetent adults with whom he lived. Because men do not have the equipment necessary for breastfeeding, I had to take the breast milk from the refrigerator and warm it up before I could feed him. At the 11:00 p.m. feeding, I generally was well prepared. The 5:00 a.m. feeding, however, always started out with a groggy Aaron stumbling to the nursery, greeted by what I am sure were baby expletives calling into question all sorts of things about me. I'd scoop him up, change the diaper of a hostile baby, and make my way to the kitchen, praying that my eardrums survived this child. Once in the kitchen, I would try to heat up the milk while holding a screaming baby, who occasionally would express his anger by going as stiff as a board. I was just trying to get used to holding a new baby, and the next thing I knew, I was having to do it dead-tired while said baby seemed intent on making the job as hard as possible.

The colic also meant our little boy didn't exactly hold to the 11, 2, and 5 eating regimen. We had the hardest time getting him on a schedule because he had such issues with spitting up and his tummy. To this day I distinctly remember waking up to the sounds of a screaming baby at 3:00 a.m., rolling over, and grabbing my phone to conduct an internet search on postpartum depression in men, just in case I was experiencing symptoms.[2]

> To this day I distinctly remember waking up to the sounds of a screaming baby at 3:00 a.m., rolling over, and grabbing my phone to conduct an internet search on postpartum depression in men, just in case I was experiencing symptoms.

ELAINA SHARP CHIMES IN

[1] I can't believe you yelled at our sweet, precious, innocent baby! I say you got what you deserved.

[2] Well? Were you?

In these times, the realization that this child is a gift from God will be so important. It's why you must concentrate on it beforehand. Three a.m. is too late. As pregnancy progresses and the due date draws near, focus on this truth. God knows what He is doing, and this is from Him. He also knows that you can't do this in your own strength and that parenthood will drive you to your knees like nothing else you've ever done. In this respect, children really are the gift that keeps on giving.

SOMETHING TO PONDER

As I write this chapter, Christmas is just days away. The sounds of carols fill the air, our Christmas tree sparkles (with all the important ornaments hung at least four feet from the floor so they are out of the reach of the 18-month-old Jedi), and our home is abuzz with the excitement of the season. One of the things that has always struck me about the Christmas story is the small verse of Luke 2:19. The New American Standard Bible's translation—"But Mary treasured all these things, pondering them in her heart"—is typical of English translations. The Message renders it, "Mary kept all these things to herself, holding them dear, deep within herself." Mary was a virgin who had just given birth to God in the flesh. The Son of God came to earth as a human baby, and because she had found favor with God, Mary was the one chosen to bear the God-man. Luke 2:19 comes just after she has given birth to Jesus and placed Him in a manger. As if that wasn't surreal enough, the baby in a manger then receives His first visitors: a bunch of stinky, smelly shepherds who had been informed of His birth by an angelic choir. This is the context of Mary noticing every little detail and committing it to memory.

It would be fair to say Mary's experience was vastly different than that of any other soon-to-be-parent in history. Yet I think there is something here for every parent. You have no idea how many times God will bless you with a child. And no matter how many children you are blessed with, you will only give birth to each child one time. This is a unique, once-in-a-lifetime experience. You will never get it back. Real life doesn't have a rewind or a pause button, and this fact will only become more pronounced as that little baby grows up.

> This is a unique, once-in-a-lifetime experience. You will never get it back. Real life doesn't have a rewind or a pause button, and this fact will only become more pronounced as that little baby grows up.

There will be so much about life that you cannot control. Sickness, school bullies, broken hearts, dashed dreams, failures, and missed shots. Aced tests, victories, successes, perfect recitals, true love, and game-winning goals.[3] But before the baby comes, all of that is in the distant future. Right now, in this moment, everything is new, and the truth that an amazing, all-powerful, perfect God chose you for this mission is staring you right in the face. Soon it will probably spit up in your face too.[4]

Take the time to remember every detail you can, but don't beat yourself up later if you can't remember something. Take the time to look around the delivery room. Don't rush through those last few doctor's appointments if you can help it. Yes, you are busy, and if you are like we were, you have jobs, other kids, and all sorts of things going on. But do your best to slow down and take it all in. Pregnancy is a hard road, but it is a road you don't know how often you will travel, and far too quickly it is a road you won't travel again.

> Soak it all in. Immerse yourself in the moment. Keep all these things to yourself, and hold them dear, deep within yourself.

Soak it all in. Immerse yourself in the moment. Keep all these things to yourself, and hold them dear, deep within yourself.

Now all you have to do is take care of a baby, which is another book altogether.

ELAINA SHARP CHIMES IN

[3] Baby snuggles, neck hugs, hand-holding, and belly laughs. Are you sure we can't have another baby?

[4] And even in your mouth, if truth be told. Don't make the mistake of thinking it won't happen to you.

MORE GREAT HARVEST HOUSE BOOKS FOR DADS

Dad Tired and Loving It
Jerrad Lopes

Join a new generation of Christian husbands and fathers who want to be better spiritual leaders than their fathers were. Get equipped and encouraged in your day-to-day life as you strive to be the man God is calling you to be—even when you're dad tired.

The Perfect Dad
Rob Stennett

Father-of-four Rob Stennett isn't the perfect dad, and neither are you—but that doesn't have to stop you from trying to be the best father you can possibly be. Discover the 12 essential roles in a dad's job description that will help train you for parenthood.

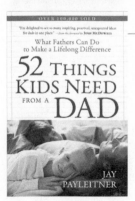

52 Things Kids Need from a Dad
Jay Payleitner

This empowering confidence builder includes creative, doable ideas for building relationships with your kids; step-up-to-the-mark challenges; encouraging ways to be an example and create a legacy…and *no* long lists or criticism for acting like a man.

52 Things Daughters Need from Their Dads
Jay Payleitner

Jay guides you into "girl land," offering ways to do things *with* your daughter, not just *for* them; lecture less and listen more; be alert for "hero moments"; and give your daughter a positive view of the male sex. You'll gain confidence in building lifelong positives into your girl.

52 Things Sons Need from Their Dads
Jay Payleitner

These 52 quick-to-read chapters offer a bucketful of man-friendly ideas on building a father-son relationship. By your life and example, you can show your boy how to work hard and have fun, often at the same time; live with honesty and self-respect; and develop the inner confidence to live purposefully.

To learn more about Harvest House books and
to read sample chapters, visit our website:

www.harvesthousepublishers.com

HARVEST HOUSE PUBLISHERS
EUGENE, OREGON